Praise for the Book

———◆▸✦◂◆———

This book takes the foundation of attachment theory and brings it alive in the face of the most challenging behaviours that parents may face when parenting children with early attachment disruption histories. Rather than focusing on behaviours, Post goes into the very root of the cause and gives parents simple and concise guidance on how to respond in a manner that will help re-establish secure attachment where it may once have been lost.

— Sir Richard Bowlby

The Great Behavior Breakdown addresses the most difficult behaviors that parents can face. It gives parents an eye-opening and heart-opening understanding of the causes of these behaviors, and a practical way to work with them that puts the focus on strengthening the relationship rather than trying to control the behavior.

Like the best medicine, it addresses the root problems and not just the symptoms. We all love our children, but making that love real in the eye of the storm can be extremely challenging. This book will teach you about your own stress reactions, and how you can respond more effectively to your children from your own inner strength with compassionate understanding, rather than reacting out of your fear.

— Myla Kabat-Zinn, co-author of *Everyday Blessings: The Inner Work of Mindful Parenting*

Bryan's book provides insights, techniques and real world tools to help parents understand their child's trauma and stresses. The book is insightful and a must read for all parents.

— Bren Wolfe, Founder, www.JourneyToMe.com

After reading the Great Behavior Breakdown, I found the ultimate tool for my toolbox. This book covers all the toughest behaviors and uses language that is easy to understand. I have recommended it to numerous families and have received positive feedback about the ease of implementing these tools as well as how helpful it is to understand the stress underlying the behavior. This is one of the most helpful books I've read. I recommend it for any person involved with children; therapists, parents, and educators.

— Stacy G. York, LCSW, www.stacyyork.com

This book is so powerful and has an immense value. It is an essential resource for all parents and professionals working with children and their families. Dr. Post's expertise is shared in such a way that can be understood by all. The most powerful aspect is that it assists parents to return to our most precious God-given gift—unconditional love. I greatly appreciate the empowerment provided to parents in assisting them to be the most important catalyst for change and healing with their children.

— Kimberly Erickson-Nichols, MS, APSW, LPC
www.heart-to-hearthealing.com

This book, this model, has changed my life and the lives of those around me. As I evolve more and more into a place of love and regulation, I feel the unlimited benefits of connection in my relationships and peace in my life. Thank you, Dr. Post, for your extraordinary courage to offer love in the midst of fear and pain.

— Lisa Boyles, LPC, www.healingforthefamily.com

COMMENTS ABOUT BRYAN POST FROM PARENTS AND PROFESSIONALS

Bryan goes beyond "Beyond Consequences, Logic and Control" by including strategies for more difficult behaviors. He continues to be a master at simplifying the complicated. The Great Behavior Breakdown is a user friendly guide for healing and life change. It is not for the faint of heart, that is, those who wish to hold onto their old paradigms. Experience how putting love into action heals relationships and extinguishes negative behaviors. Bryan's work is revolutionizing the way we need to parent our children.

—Ken Thom, MS, LPC is a Christian parenting expert who uses Scripture and Biblical truths along with the Post Institute Stress Model to put love into action to heal relationships. Ken is available for parent and therapist coaching and is a certified BCI parent trainer. He can be reached at thomkt@embarqmail.com or through kenthomcounseling.com.

Powerful, humbling, revolutionary, sensible, outstanding! Your theory is challenging on so many levels...my goal in life is to be able to fully embrace and integrate these principles. Everything in my being tells me this is the way to create harmony in my family. The challenge I face is overcoming the years of fear and traditional thinking about the intentions of my children.

—C. Ellis, CA

Thank you for your professionalism, your intuitiveness, and academic profoundness. I really appreciate the work you encourage us to do as couples. The concept of the parents creating the path for

healing in our family makes so much sense and speaks to my heart.
—A. Turner, CA

What an eye opener! I have gone from tolerating my sons to really enjoying them. I would recommend your approach to everyone including educators. I am really learning a lot about myself, and my family.
—A. Allen, VA

Thank you for reinforcing what we've known all along in our hearts. We had lost our way and are on the right path again. I am certain we will continue to benefit from this enlightening information.
—K. Jones, WA

Bryan, Your insight on parenting is 100% right on the money. It has allowed me to approach my child from an entirely new understanding of how to understand his needs and meet them from a place of emotional health, peace, and love.
—S. Kervin, VA

Fantastic Information! Thank you soooo much!! Hard work, but very eye opening. Simple ideas, but not easy to put into practice. I am learning how easy it is to get caught up in fear, and the importance of daily focus to integrate this new paradigm.
—O. Perry, OK

When I read all the challenges that people face raising children with trauma history I feel guilty getting frustrated with my 4-year-old's limited meltdowns! All of Dr. Post's work has been helpful to me as a parent as well as in my professional work. I certainly thought I knew a lot about raising children until I had my own. Thanks for everything you do to assist parents!
—Kelly J, VA

Hey Bryan,

I have to tell you that I have referred countless struggling parents to your resources, especially the DVD series on healing the attachment challenged child. There is little/no training for adoptive families adopting internationally and while it would seem obvious that of course kids coming out of a war-torn country and living in extreme poverty/abuse would have stress-related behaviors, most parents are completely overwhelmed. 3 of our children were adopted from disruptions, and unfortunately that is very common as parents aren't aware of how their child's behaviors are triggering their own unresolved "stuff" and starting that negative feed-back loop rooted in fear.

We've also had several teenagers live with us, runaways from group homes, kids in and out of treatment centers, etc. and again, your materials have been immensely helpful. I speak to stressed out foster/adoptive parents every day, occasionally at conferences, and I am always referring them to your materials and they have all been blessed. We've also been able to share your materials with stressed out single moms living in poverty who need help dealing with their children's rage.

I am on a task force here in Iowa called CRTEC which is the "Center to Restore Trafficked and Exploited Children" which is training up families to foster/adopt children rescued out of the sex industry both domestically and abroad. Again, your resources were the first I recommended for people to get a picture of the affect of trauma on the brain and behaviors.

Thank you for what you are doing. Helping people get to the root instead of focusing on the rotten fruit is major. Seeing past behavior and into the frightened child within has helped countless families in our area come back from the brink of hopelessness and experience the peace and joy that families were designed to live in. Thank you!

—Love, Jenny G. Marion, IA

I saw your DVD that changed my whole outlook on life. I began watching this as a Dad that was all but turning my back on the two older kids. I wanted them back but under many conditions. After watching your program, I lost all conditions and became very proactive in the return of these two children that we will be adopting.

—With Courageous Love, Dr Patrick Gilmer Citrus Springs, FL

I have a caseload of 16 children right now; they have all come into foster care due to abuse and / or neglect, parental rights have been terminated, and they are free for adoption. Most of my 16 munchkins have some very, very challenging issues. I found out about Dr. Post's work through another source. I listened to some of his CDs and was hooked. I have recommended them to most of the foster parents who care for my kids. I very often see foster parents using interventions that just do not work. Unfortunately, this is very common, and very frustrating!! I am also in my last semester of school to earn a master's in counseling psychology, so I am interested in Dr. Post's work as both an adoption worker and counselor.

—CT, Stephenville TX

The Great Behavior Breakdown

B. Bryan Post

THE GREAT BEHAVIOR BREAKDOWN
By B. Bryan Post

Published by Post Institutes & Associates, LLC, Palmyra VA
www.postinstitute.com

Post Publishing Division's Books, DVDs and Audio training programs are available at special quantity discounts for use in corporate, government or agency training programs. For more information please call 434-589-8828 or write to Director of Special Sales and Training, Post Publishing Division, 2819 Haden Martin Road, Palmyra, VA 22963 (email david@postinstitute.com). Or contact your local bookstore. Online Training programs are also offered through www.postinstitute.com.

Library of Congress Control Number:

ISBN: 978-0-9840801-0-6

Interior Design by Jon Marken

Cover Design by December Design Inc., www.decemberdesignsinc.com

Third Printing March 2013

OTHER WORKS BY THE AUTHOR

BOOKS:
Beyond Consequences, Logic, and Control: A Love-Based Approach for Helping Children with Severe Behaviors (Co-authored with Heather Forbes)
From Fear to Love: Parenting Difficult Adopted Children
For All Things a Season
Going Home: A Survival Toolkit for Parents (Co-authored with Sue Grantham)
Healing Adult Attachment Handbook Vol. 1
How to End Lying Now!
How to Heal the Attachment Challenged, Angry and Defiant Child: When Behavior Modification and Consequences Don't Work (Workbook)
Parenting Softly: From Infant to Two
The Forever Child: A Tale of Fear and Anger (Co-authored with Nancy Clark)
The Forever Child: A Tale of Lies and Love (Co-authored with Nancy Clark)
The Forever Child: A Tale of Loss and Impossible Dreams (Co-authored with Nancy Clark)
The Great Behavior Breakdown

DVDs, CDs & ONLINE COURSES:
Adoption Subsidy and the Law: What Every Parent Needs to Know (CD Audio Recording)
Art of the Family–Centered Therapist: Fear and the Dance Between Therapist and Client (CD Audio Recording)
Bryan Post's Adult Attachment Seminars (CD Audio Recording)
Creating Healing for the Attachment Challenged Adult (CD/DVD)
Dr. Bryan for the Family Live Radio Show (11 CD Audio Recording)
Educating Children Today: Working with the Difficult Child in the Classroom (DVD)
Effective Strategies for Severe Behaviors in Adoptive and Foster Children (DVD)
Family Regulatory Therapy for the Attachment Challenged Adult, Child and Family (DVD)
Getting Started with Bryan Post: A Journey toward the Family-Centered Way for Parents (CD Audio Recording)

Healing Adult Attachment Disorder (CD Audio Recording)
Holiday Peace: How to Turn the Stressful Holidays Into Peaceful Family Time
   (CD Audio Recording)
*How to Heal the Attachment Challenged, Angry and Defiant Child: When
   Behavior Modification and Consequences Don't Work* (CD/DVD)
Parenting Attachment Challenged Children "Hands-On" Home Study Course
IEP's and the Law: What Every Parent Needs to Know. (CD Audio
   Recording)
International Adoption Course Ages Birth to Five (12 CD Audio Recording)
Stress, Love & Your Baby's Developing Brain: Understanding How Your
   Parenting Approach Influences Your Baby's Brain Development From
   Prenatal to Two. *(DVD)*
Stress, Trauma, and the Secret Life of Your Child (CD Audio Recording)
The Great Behavior Breakdown (13 CD Audio Recording)
*Understanding & Meeting the 9 Most Important Emotional Needs for Foster
   & Adopted Children* (DVD)

Many of our programs are available online in our e-Learning Center
for immediate viewing or listening to at reduced prices. Visit http://
postinstitute.com/elearn.

TABLE OF CONTENTS

BABY BLUES © BABY
BLUES PARTNERSHIP.
KING FEATURES
SYNDICATE

DEDICATION

——◆◆┼╳┼◆◆——

This book is dedicated to all of my Post Institute Parents, knowing that every day you are striving to be more mindful, present and loving. In the face of some of the most challenging behaviors parents face, you are not giving up, but giving in to love.

Thank you for being a part of the Love Revolution!

Choose Love,
B.

Acknowledgements

All honor goes first and foremost to my ever loving God. It is 2014 and I cannot possibly say enough for what God has done in my life. I am a grateful man. In my prayers I always start with the Our Father and then my very next words are how very grateful I am. I am grateful for every moment I've experienced, the painful and pleasant. My Lord continues to work with me in every moment and even more than that provides for me the most beautiful, loving example of who I want to be and the light I want to shine in the world. For that, I thank God.

Next, I want to thank my mother, Opal Post. We have been through so much since I first recorded the audio program for The Great Behavior Breakdown. I recorded that program from home while my father lay dying in our living room, sick with cancer. Those were difficult times for our family. And sadly, it didn't end with the loss of my father. Just three years later my amazing grandmother passed away, and three years after her passing my sister, Kristi, was killed in a car wreck. Needless to say, it's been quite a journey and it has sure taken a toll on my mother. Every step of the way she's only gotten stronger in her faith and her love for me just grows stronger. I am so thankful for this woman and the impact she's had on my life.

I can't possibly see this book going for another reprinting without acknowledging my dear friends and partners, David and Susan Durovy. I can't express the impact they've had on my life, the support, and source of constancy they have provided. For an attachment challenged adult such as myself, it means the world. Without the two of them there is the greatest likelihood that The Great Behavior Breakdown wouldn't have made it through even its second printing.

A special thanks to all of the GBB Certified Instructors who continue to bring this message to the world.

Finally, a special thanks to my family. My beautiful and talented wife Tammy and our son Donnie. The gift that started my parenting journey as a scared and overwhelmed twenty-one year old, Mikalah. You make me so proud. And her great mother Tige. My amazing and gifted daughter Marley and her mother Kristi, for continuing to love and accept me even when I stumble and struggle. And my son Kevin, whom I am very proud of and who is also making me a grandfather! And to my other "kids", who God has blessed me to love and guide over the years, you know who you are!

FOREWORD

I am honored to write this foreword for my friend Bryan Post. I know some of you may have heard that this man is too controversial to make a real contribution to our field of helping parents raise traumatized children. It is for this reason that perhaps he has more to contribute than most. I would like to submit for your consideration that you might have this opinion simply because you have not sat down and read Bryan's work.

My writing this foreword is to ask you to read this book. *The Great Behavior Breakdown* is one of the best books written about parenting traumatized children that I have read since the first book Bryan co-authored *Beyond Consequences, Logic, and Control Vol. 1*. The combination of both books make up the best work I have read in my nearly 25 year career helping parents raise the traumatized older children that I have placed with them for adoption.

Why am I so gung-ho about *The Great Behavior Breakdown?* Bryan advocates a sincerely loving approach to parenting traumatized children. Bryan illustrates the point that the reason it is so difficult to raise traumatized children is because of the way many of us were parented. For so many of us, the parenting role model we had did not prepare us for raising traumatized children or teenagers (both teens adopted as teens and our own birth teens.)

What I like most about *The Great Behavior Breakdown* is that it advocates a form of parenting that we all wished was modeled on us when we were children and particularly when we were teenagers. We needed parents who used patience, understanding, kindness, and empathy and, yes, even love as a means to teach us to face life's challenges. We all needed parents who would spend time with us when we were feeling our lowest. We all needed parents who could have given us "time in" rather than "time out." We all needed parents who could contain us while treating us with the compassion that we needed in our moments of being out of control. We needed parents who used the power of their example rather than choose to control us; whether it was by corporal punishment, ridicule, consequences, or simply making it clear to us that we were not worthy of their approval unless we succeeded on their terms.

If you are a parent who is having a difficult time dealing with your child's severe behavior give Bryan Post's combined works *Beyond Consequences, Logic, and Control Part I* and this great parenting primer *The Great Behavior Breakdown* a chance. Read them slowly. Absorb what he is saying. Read it a few times. Be prepared to change the way you look at parenting and rededicate yourself to spending more positive time with your acting out child.

If you are a professional who needs some unique ideas about how to work with families who are dealing with children who have severe behaviors please keep your mind open and read Bryan's work. *The Great Behavior Breakdown* offers parents and professionals alike a framework for a more satisfying, committed and healthy parent child relationship.

Pat O'Brien, MS, LMSW
Founder & Executive Director
You Gotta Believe! The Older Child Adoption & Permanency Movement, Inc.
ygbpat@msn.com; www.yougottabelieve.org; 718-372-3003.

On Life in the Trenches

(For this reprinting David, my partner, asked if I wanted to keep Life in the Trenches as is. After reading it I can't imagine leaving it out but at the same time in the name of transparency I need to give you an update. After another six months we were able to reconnect Lakasha with her biological family who she had not seen or heard from in over ten years. Not to mention several months after that her mother, whom she had also not seen or heard from in ten years, was also being released from prison. Shortly after reconnecting with her biological family LaKasha went to live with them. We stayed in contact for another six months or so but have since lost contact. Kristi and I eventually moved back to Oklahoma, where we are both from, to try to breathe in some good country air after our time in Virginia. However, after all of the dust settled a couple of years later we ended up divorcing. Primarily it was my choice. The children I write about are no different than me. Even as an adult who has been teaching and writing about this work for over fifteen years, every day can still sometimes be a struggle. Thank God these days I have far more good days than not so good, but at any given moment I can drop into my fear and stress sensitivity which also drives the children of this book. My hope is that this book can guide you early in your relationship with your child. That is actually my only hope...that it will equip you to communicate with your child in a way that he may understand himself sooner as opposed to later. I believe that makes all of the difference. God Bless.)

My friend Helene Timpone called on my wife Kristi's behalf to tell me she was having problems at home. I called...no answer. I called again...still no answer. I sent her a text message to make sure everything was okay, and she replied, "Now!" It became pretty clear that all was *not* okay and I sped home, of course all the time thinking the worst. (Remember that in times of stress our thinking becomes confused and distorted.) Since I was still ten minutes away, I asked one of my former star healing home parents, who lives around the block, to go over and check on things. He made it before I did. Shortly thereafter Kristi called to let me know that everything was okay.

What I saw when I walked in was hard to digest: Our house was 80% wrecked. I am saying 80% in the most honest assessment. From the sunroom to the kitchen to the living room, office space, hallway, and bathroom, there was very little left standing. Shaving cream was smeared on the walls, all of my daughter's arts and crafts were strewn about, the computer, stereo, and lamp were in a heap, and the computer screen was destroyed. The house smelled sour because the contents of the fridge were all over the floor, the trash was dumped, the cabinets and drawers were completely emptied. Pictures were broken, glass was everywhere, thumbtacks, nails, towels, name it!

We'd had a 19-year-old young lady living with us for the past couple of months. She has spent most of her life in residential treatment centers and therapeutic foster care. Children don't "grow up" in facilities, they only get bigger. After failed attempts for this young lady to be assimilated into the community, she eventually signed herself out of care only to find she had nowhere to go. How does this become my problem? Well, it's actually all of our problem, for we are all connected. As we continue to turn our backs on children like this, we only add to humanity's miserable condition. I do more than my share in this area. I run a group home that takes only the most difficult and challenging of Virginia's foster children, all of whom have failed in other placements. Mind you: I didn't say *one* of them, I said *all* of them. And we are loving each and every one into a peaceful existence.

I typically guard my home life well. Having spent a number of years somewhat of a public figure, when I can I like to retreat into obscurity—my home being one such oasis. But life is bigger than my need for privacy. And I've been Pat O'Brien'd! Once you've been Pat O'Brien'd, your perspective on children and homelessness changes. You can't help but get involved at a greater level. Nevertheless, my 19-year-old had a moment in failed verbal communication and she expressed herself the only way she knew how. She wrecked the house while Kristi watched. Eventually Harold showed up and took her out of the house to get something to eat.

When I arrived I was quite upset. Most don't get to see me upset. It's more an energetic state than it is a physical look; when I'm upset, you can *feel* it. I called Harold and asked where he had taken her; they were at McDonald's down the road. I asked him to put her on the phone and told her, "Get your food and get home and help clean up this damn mess!" She hung up on me. Later she texted and said she wasn't coming back to our f&#@king house and that I could kiss her a#%. I texted her back and said, "Oh yeah you gonna come back even if I have to put you in the trunk!" She said she was gonna call the cops.

When I arrived, I asked her if we needed to wait for the police to arrive; she said they hadn't been called. I asked her if she wanted me to call them, she stated no. I said get in the car. She got in the car. I took her home. All of the way home we "processed"— meaning I yelled at her that she was not going to leave like every other home she had been in after she had torn it up (this behavior is a common pattern), and furthermore I was not going to call the police (as she had encouraged my wife to do in the midst of destroying the house), and she was going to help clean up because this was now her home.

Was I mad? Absolutely, but not in a blaming way—in a passionate way that says, "Throw it at me, throw it all at me because it's not until you are through throwing that you and I are gonna trust that this is real." Did I yell? Absolutely—not in a blaming or threatening way, but rather in a way that said this is exactly where I stand and how I feel, I'm not gonna leave you guessing. Did I feel like hurting her back? You bet I did. Once I went through the house and saw that every room was wrecked except for hers, I had the impulse to trash her room also. I did not, but I felt like it. Did I doubt my ability and desire to love this child? Most certainly. The thoughts flow like water during those moments. That's okay and normal. It's your commitment, understanding, and relationship that has to help you turn off that faucet—then you move on.

What would I have done had I been home when she was wrecking the house? We live fifty feet from the ocean; I probably would have dragged us both into the icy cold water and dunked her until she woke up, because love exists—sometimes we just have to be woken out of our sleep.

And what, Bryan, of consequences? There are both natural and parent-formulated consequences. Let the parent-formulated ones go. Stay with the natural ones. She destroyed the computer screen, so no MySpace. She destroyed the phone, so no phone. I have both a laptop and a cell phone, as does my wife, so we are fine! Eventually, she will replace both, as her allowance permits, but until then she will have to figure something else out and every impulse to be on the phone or the computer is met by the inherent shame of having torn up her opportunities. That needs no shaming or guilting from me; it's just a natural byproduct of behavior.

After a while, she helped the best that she could. We slowly got the place picked up. We are moving into a bigger house soon, so this just gave us a head start. I was scheduled to be at the group home overnight, so before leaving I gave her a hug, told her I loved her, hugged my wife, and was off to work.

There will be more to come, and the growth is mine to be had. As I grow, I learn and see more, deeper, clearer, with more wisdom. I am thankful for this opportunity.

ॐ

I am now thankful that you are reading this book. Each of the behaviors addressed is to many parents the equivalent of having my house wrecked. Each is challenging, frustrating, and certainly make you question your sanity and why on earth you are trying to parent this child. Most give up, opting to place their child in residential treatment centers in the hopes they will get better, though most do not or, worse, the families give up on the child.

Behavior expression is the only form of communication that a child has learned up to this point. If she knew another way I trust she would use it. She does not, she has never been taught it, thus now must be taught it and must learn it to use it. *If you didn't get it, you don't have it, and you gotta get it.*

In this book I have given very specific steps for helping your child break through some of the most challenging behaviors that you as a parent will ever face. Conquer one and I am certain others will arise—but with love, understanding, faith, passion, and commitment you will make it through to the other side. Do not give up.

It's been six months now since the story I recounted above. There have been no other wrecked house episodes, but there have been more episodes, some more scary than others. Nevertheless, my family is growing and so, too, is this young woman by being a part of it.

May God abundantly bless you with love and wisdom as you read these pages and move forward into the healing of your child's heart.

B.

Introduction

When children exhibit disturbing or difficult behaviors, we often feel at a loss. We may seek professional help, but when that doesn't work, what do we do? It can be very distressing, and many parents end up feeling there's no hope. Families crumble under the pressure, and relationships are damaged. But it doesn't have to be that way.

The techniques you will read in this book have proven effective in 92.6% of cases where a therapist or parent has implemented them consistently for at least two weeks.[1] This is **The Great Behavior Breakdown challenge.** If you implement the information you read in this book for just two weeks, I guarantee a 50% dramatic reduction, if not elimination, of your child's behavior. If you implement the information for 30 days or more, the results will be dramatic.

How to Use This Book

This Introduction and Chapter 1 contain important information that will help you understand the principles of the techniques that follow. Read these two sections over and over in order to integrate and fully take in this information. Repetition is very important in order to truly understand the concepts.

Then, you may skip forward to the chapter that pertains to your child's specific behavior. However, you may find it interesting to read all of the chapters. If your child ever exhibits one of the other

---

[1] Results of 2003 study conducted by the Post Institute for Family-Centered Therapy involving 20 parents of children demonstrating severe behaviors. Testing utilized an informal 5 point Likert scale. Of the 20 parents: 17 completed the pre/post test measure; 1 incomplete; 2 did not respond.

behaviors, you'll have a head start in knowing how to deal with the situation. Plus, you'll have a very comprehensive view of how these techniques work, which will enable you to handle your job as a parent much better from moment to moment to moment.

A Paradigm Shift

Our immediate tendency is to reject anything new. We've been taught to see children and their behaviors in a certain way, and change is never easy. You may find that these concepts are very different from your customary way of thinking. For this reason, they may be difficult for you to accept at first. What's required is a paradigm shift—a new perspective.

We spend a lot of time *expanding* our paradigms, but rarely do we *challenge* our dominant paradigms. Dr. Spock changed his paradigm when he was in his 80's. He came to believe that he had contributed to the traumatization of a nation by encouraging parents to let their babies cry themselves to sleep. He realized that he had been wrong and completely altered his thinking.

The truth is that it does no good to hold onto concepts that are wrong simply because they're comfortable. But it takes willingness and effort to embrace new concepts. It takes repetition and emotional impact. You must become educated and develop new awareness, and you must develop a complete understanding of the new information. Then, you must apply that information every single day. All of the techniques in this book are built on the foundation of repetition, repetition, repetition. Emotional impact occurs when you see the techniques working or when you feel it in your bones. Something may happen that makes that light bulb immediately go off in your head.

I know that it can be very scary to change something you've always thought was true, but all I'm asking is that you try these techniques for two weeks. If you've been struggling with your child's behaviors for weeks, months, or years, what do you have to lose? Just try it on. You don't have to buy.

You must, however, take the time to understand the concepts in order to apply them. Action without understanding only leads back to confusion. For example, you may believe that your child's behavior is abnormal, but we only view something as abnormal when we don't understand it. When we understand something, it ceases to be abnormal. Once you understand the unconscious motivations for your child's behavior, you'll no longer see the behavior as abnormal, and you'll finally be able to help your child. That's why I recommend reading the introductory chapters several times and reading the entire book even if your child only exhibits one of the behaviors covered. You'll drink in the information, and once you have an understanding, you will be able to create your own solutions as problems arise.

THE STRESS MODEL

The techniques in this book are based on a Stress Model, which explains the root cause of problematic behavior. It is the core of everything else you will read in this book. If you can't embrace the three foundational principles of the Stress Model, it will be hard to apply the information in this book. So, refer to this model often, and remind yourself frequently of the three principles. In fact, if you're able to fully grasp the Stress Model and the wide-ranging implications of its applicability, you will be able to create a healing dynamic for your family within the next moment!

The three principles of the Stress Model are as follows:

> **Principle #1: All behaviors arise from a state of stress.**
> In between the behavior and the stress is the presence of a primary emotion. It is through the expression, the processing, and the understanding of that emotion that we can calm the stress and diminish the behavior.

> **Principle #2: There are only two primary emotions: *love and fear*.** This may be hard to grasp because we iden-

tify a large spectrum of emotions, but any emotion or behavior that isn't loving stems from a root of fear. You may see frustration, anger, jealousy, hurt, sadness, or anxiety, or you may see behaviors such as self-mutilation and stealing. But they all stem from fear. Examine your own emotions, and you'll discover this is true. None of us act out in a negative way when we're feeling the emotion of love. Hence, children's negative behaviors are driven from a place of fear.

Principle #3: Children with severe behaviors DO NOT CONSCIOUSLY CHOOSE to act out that behavior. These behaviors are driven from a highly *unconscious* place.

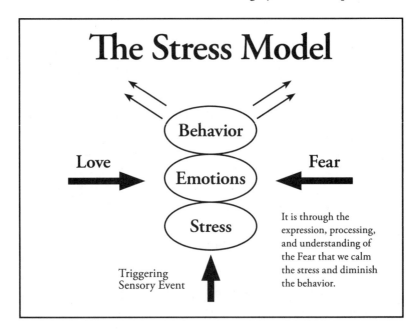

DYSREGULATION

According to Bruce Perry, M.D., we all respond to stress in one of two different ways. We either become hyper-aroused or hypo-aroused, which are just different ways of reacting to stress. So, what's the difference between hyper- and hypo-arousal? Either sex can exhibit either state of arousal, but girls tend to go into hypo-arousal. Stress makes them behave with defiance, resistance, depression, and withdrawal. Boys tend to become hyper-aroused, which leads to anger, hyperactive behavior, and hyper-vigilance.

In the stress state—whether hyper-aroused or hypo-aroused— **our thinking processes become confused and distorted, and our short-term memory is suppressed.** This stress state is called **dysregulation.** Our behavior is an attempt to bring ourselves back to a state of regulation, which is a calmer state, no longer in stress overload. That's why calming the stress diminishes the behavior, and that's what each chapter in this book will teach you how to do—**calm your child's stress level (as well as your own) in order to diminish or eliminate the behavior.**

Regulation doesn't necessarily mean the absence of stress. Some degree of stress is pertinent to your healthy growth and development, but too much stress will leave you trapped in a state of fear. Regulation, then, is the state of stress within your window of tolerance. We all have our own window of tolerance. If the stress you experience is within your tolerance level, you can maintain regulation.

Dysregulation occurs when you experience stress that is outside of or greater than your window of tolerance. As adults, we have a regulatory system that often allows us to quickly bring our level of stress back into our window of tolerance. For some children (and probably some adults you know as well), the window of tolerance is very small. If the child has experienced trauma, it can be smaller than you may have ever imagined. **By applying these techniques, you can begin to increase your child's window of tolerance and ability to regulate.**

If your child is chronically acting out or misbehaving, the child is attempting to communicate to you that he or she is in a state of fear and overwhelming stress that cannot be stopped without parental assistance. It may seem illogical that a child would attempt to regulate himself or herself through destructive behavior, but remember that the child is operating from a very unconscious place. How logical are you capable of staying when you're stressed out?

THE FOUR LEVELS OF MEMORY

Another important concept is that there are four levels of memory: cognitive, emotional, motor, and state. A great reference for more on levels of memory is Bruce D. Perry, M.D. of www.childtrauma academy.org.

1. Cognitive is mental memory.
2. Emotional is, of course, emotional memory.
3. Motor memory is in the body.
4. The State level of memory is where trauma settles, and it's the deepest and most unconscious level of memory.

90% of our emotional memory is unconscious, while 100% of motor memory and 100% of state level memory are unconscious.

Think about this concept for a moment. Motor memory is unconscious because you aren't aware from moment to moment of your body's functions. You aren't consciously aware of the beating of your heart, for example, and you aren't even consciously aware of all of the things your body does when you're driving a car. Unless we make a very diligent effort to be otherwise through the practice of mindfulness as taught by Jon and Myla Kabat-Zinn in their wonderful book *Everyday Blessings: The Inner Work of Mindful Parenting*, we are largely unaware of our emotions from moment to moment.

Traumatic memories reside in the state level of memory, which also remains unconscious unless we make a concerted effort to bring that memory into consciousness. Bringing the light of consciousness to that unconscious place is where healing can take place. That's what allows for regulation and changes in behavior.

When something happens that triggers the state level of memory, it directs all other levels of memory. This is important to understand. This is why your child's behavior is unconscious. There is no conscious decision to drive you crazy. So, if we look at the fundamental mechanisms for how we behave when we're triggered into stress and when the state level is activated, we realize that the behavior is very much an unconscious process.

When we encounter a novel event or stimuli, we perceive that event as a threat until deemed otherwise. This is the state your child experiences when the behavior manifests. When the threat is perceived, the child's "amygdala" kicks in. The amygdala is the part of the brain that responds to fear and activates the "fight or flight" response. The amygdala actually contains neurocircuitry that runs directly to your gut. This is why you have a gut feeling or perhaps even irritable bowel syndrome.

It has only been 15 years since psychologists recognized that our initial reaction to a threat is not actually fight or flight. Our first reaction is to *freeze*. If the door slams, you don't immediately slap the person standing next to you, right? You freeze first and then determine if you need to fight or flee. Our initial reaction is not to attack; it's to survive. Your child's unconscious might say, "If I'm not frozen, I must fight. Therefore, when you come toward me, I have to attack you. Otherwise, you will hurt me." In times of stress, the cells of our bodies literally constrict into survival.

The hippocampus is another part of the brain which is the upper level thinking process. This part of the brain can evaluate a situation and determine that there is no threat. For adults, this evaluation usually happens in a matter of milliseconds. For a child, particularly a child with a trauma history, this evaluation may not be possible without some positive intervention from you. That's largely what this book is all about.

While the amygdala develops in the first 18 months of life, the hippocampus doesn't complete its development until after 36 months. So, the baby isn't capable on a very real neurologic level of calming itself down. It needs the parent to do that, and the parent's effectiveness in regulating the baby's stress will have a lot to do with how well that baby's brain develops. Studies show that children who have been neglected have smaller brains. Children with normal development are better able to regulate themselves when they experience stress than children with a trauma history. Their window of tolerance is, quite literally, larger.

Now, you know why Dr. Spock took back his earlier directive about letting children cry themselves to sleep. After his book, we learned that babies are virtually incapable of self-regulating.

John Bowlby, the Father of Attachment Theory, stated that the first three years of our lives create a blueprint for the rest of our lives. In his seminal work *Affect Regulation and the Origin of the Self,* modern day attachment pioneer Allan Schore shares a shocking scientific finding that *"affect dysregulation (the lack of ability to calm ourselves down) is seen to be a fundamental mechanism in all psychiatric disorders" (Taylor, et. al. 1997).* The efficiency of each person's regulatory system will determine how well they can maintain relationships with others.

So, you can take a child out of the traumatic situation, but rarely do children get out of the trauma themselves. It doesn't matter how many years ago the actual trauma occurred because that trauma impacted this child's ability to regulate. **The cells of our bodies hold trauma lifelong.** There's some belief that sexual abuse prevents some mechanisms in the brain from regenerating. Neglect appears to cause the worst kind of impact. It doesn't even matter if you adopt a child right out of the womb, there may still be a traumatic impact. According to Physician Mitch Gaynor, author of *The Sounds of Healing,* as early as the fourth week after conception, the fetus is already capable of auditory processing. Pre and Peri-natal pioneering psychiatrist Thomas Verny says that as early as the second trimester, the fetus is already capable of psychological processing. Meaning that while still in the womb the fetus is actually thinking about experiences happening both inside and outside of the womb.

A woman I spoke with told me she had been terrified of birds as long as she could remember. A bird flew down on her car one day, and she had an immediate *freeze* reaction. She literally couldn't move. Suddenly, she remembered that she had seen her sister attacked by a chicken when she was just 7 years old. That's the power of traumatic experiences.

A traumatic event is any stressful event that is prolonged, overwhelming, or unpredictable. When such events go on unexpressed, unprocessed, and misunderstood, that makes the difference between short-term trauma and long-term trauma.

DISCIPLINE, NOT PUNISHMENT

The word "discipline" has come to mean punishment, but the origin of the word is quite different. Discipline comes from the word "disciple" which has nothing at all to do with punishment. It's all about teaching.

If your child's behavior is the result of stress, how can punishment work? It will only increase your child's stress, which will, in turn, only increase the behavior you're trying to alleviate. When the child is lost in a state level, no teaching can take place. Remember that when we're in that unconscious stress state, our thought processes are confused and distorted, and short-term memory is suppressed. So, whatever actions you take while your child is dysregulated will have no positive effect. In fact, your child probably won't even be capable of remembering what you said. You must move your child into a state of regulation, and only then can teaching take place.

Two things change the brain: positive relationships and a positive environment, and the positive repetition of both. The things we often consider to be positive are not positive, however. This isn't because we're intentionally trying to be negative. It's that unconsciously, we come from a fear-based emotional state. When we take action from a place of fear, it can't be accepted by anyone in a positive way. A lot of actions that we've been taught are effective parenting are actually based in fear, so they only create more stress.

The Fear Barrier

Research says that when we experience high levels of stress, we revert to an age when we experienced trauma. When adults get stressed out, they tend to act like adolescents because that was a very stressful time in their lives. You've probably said to an adult at some point, "Grow up! Act your age!" But in this instance, they *are* acting their age. It's just their emotional age rather than their chronological age.

We actually have three different ages: chronological (physical) age, cognitive age (mental capacity), and emotional age. Trauma will impact all three of these ages in some way. If a child's physicality is impacted by trauma, we can literally see it, so we recognize it. For example, you may have a 10-year-old who is the size of a 5-year-old. More than anything, however, trauma affects *emotional age.* When we say, "act your age" to a 10-year-old, the reality is that in that moment, the child's emotional age is only 3. Stress has caused the child to regress to what we call his "fear barrier." It's quite literally the best the child can do in that moment until regulation is restored.

You may take this child to a family get-together or to the mall, and he may immediately start to regress. Some children even start to babble or do silly things. Someone might say "hi" to him, and he puts his head down or turns around and snickers. All of these behaviors are the same kinds of behaviors you'd expect of a much younger child.

Children with a trauma history are more likely to have emotional, chronological, and cognitive ages that are incongruent — they don't match up. Even when they're in a semi-regulated state, these ages won't match. So, when the child moves into dysregulation, there's going to be even more incongruence between these ages.

The importance of this is that when the child is operating from the state level and is hypo- or hyper-aroused, you can't deal with that child based on his or her chronological age. You can only assess that child's emotional age and have expectations of the child based on that emotional age. So, a 10-year-old who is regressed to the age of 4 is only capable in those moments of what a 4-year-old is capable of.

Again, the child is not maliciously acting out or reverting to younger behavior as a way of manipulating you. The child is operating from a deeply unconscious state of fear and stress.

UNFINISHED BUSINESS

Working with your children using these techniques may very well require you to deal with some of your own unfinished business. **All emotional reactivity stems from unfinished business.** This means that your child's behavior may be awakening something inside you that you haven't fully dealt with. If this is the case, your own stress reaction may be even greater than someone without that unfinished business.

It is for this reason that I believe if you want to effectively treat a child, you have to work with the whole family. I always start with the parents to help them develop the ability to help their children. In 98% of all of the families I've ever worked with, the parents have had a trauma equal to if not greater than the trauma the child has experienced.

So, I'm not going to tell you that these techniques are easy, but the result is that you can begin to resolve some of your own emotional issues at the same time that you help your child. In the process, you will relieve some of your day-to-day stress, and you'll learn techniques for relaxing in the midst of tense situations. You'll certainly learn how to calm yourself down when your child is behaving in a way that normally elicits your own fear reaction.

That initial fear reaction is natural, but it's also unconscious. When you choose to *respond* rather than react, you become *response-able* and make a conscious decision as to how you will relate to emotions and behavior. You may have that initial freeze reaction, but if you have developed enough understanding, your hippocampus can then quickly kick in, telling you that there isn't any real threat.

When you react, you may rush to blame rather than take responsibility. Blame is a fear-based reaction, while choosing to be responsible means you're choosing to be aware of your own internal fear reaction. When you blame, you relinquish your control over your fear reaction and make someone else responsible for your feelings. When you're responsible, you can take a breath and respond from a conscious place that utilizes your understanding. This is what can make things better for you and your family. I've seen it over and over and over again. It really does work!

My goal is to empower parents to do what they are intuitively capable of doing. It's about reclaiming the spirit of parenting. We have a natural ability if we can regulate, calm down, and slow down. In the midst of stress, we only come up with more problems. Solutions don't come to us when we're under stress.

When you understand what is truly taking place inside your child, and you regulate yourself in order to come from love rather than fear, that's when solutions will be available to you.

———— ◆◆❋◆◆ ————

Chapter 1

EFFECTIVE TOOLS AND TECHNIQUES:
NEUROPHYSIOLOGIC FEEDBACK LOOPS,
3-PHASE INTERVENTION, TIME-IN,
AND CONTAINMENT

In this chapter, I'll share with you some specific parent-formulated techniques that are based on all of the work, research, and studying that I have done, as well as the experiences I have had in my practice. These techniques are so powerful that I have literally watched them transform relationships between parents and children overnight.

If I can communicate to you the understanding of the principles, then you can become empowered enough to come up with rapid fire solutions as situations present themselves to you. You will then be **responding instead of reacting** and perceiving the dynamics in a new way.

I have created some specific interventions, tools, and techniques that parents can use in a variety of settings for countless behaviors. These tools are going to give you immediate insight into your own reactions, how your reactions create reactions in your child, and how your child's behavior triggers an emotional reaction in you. When you can see your role in the dynamic that takes place between you and your child, you can become empowered to respond in a completely different way. This immediately shifts the environment and the dynamics in the moment. It's important for you to know as a parent that you can indeed have a dramatic impact on the situation, which allows you to live a much more peaceful life.

THE NEUROPHYSIOLOGIC FEEDBACK LOOP SYSTEM

The term "neurophysiologic" refers to both body and mind. We have body/mind feedback loops that are both positive and negative. Research has been able to determine that we communicate with one another and are connected to one another on a cellular level. In fact, every cell in our bodies contains consciousness. Is that a radical idea for you? Remember that research is bearing this out.

We call our cellular activity, functions, and communications inside us our "body consciousness." Of course, this body consciousness is *unconscious* to our minds. We're not aware moment to moment that these activities, functions, and communications are going on inside our bodies.

In his book, *The Power of Now,* Eckhart Tolle says, "Anything unconscious dissolves when you shine the light of consciousness upon it." So, what I'm talking about is shining the light of consciousness upon your cellular communications. What happens is our cells communicate through vibrations. It's the only way we communicate. Touch is powerful because it creates vibrations through the skin of another person. The words we speak create vibrations. We vibrate our communications through all of our senses—through touch, smell, eyesight, and hearing. Even the temperature of our bodies is a vibratory pattern.

Our cells vibrate, resonate, and communicate with other people. That's why physiologists say that 90% of communication is nonverbal. So, what do you communicate when your child walks toward you? What do you communicate when your child walks away from you? What do you communicate when your child goes to bed at night? Or when you go to your office? What are you communicating that doesn't come out of your mouth?

What comes out of your mouth is just the tip of the iceberg. What is really being communicated under the surface? That's powerful!

So, it's important to shine the light of consciousness on that unconscious activity. If you are really sincere and ask yourself, "What am I communicating right now?", you will get in touch with something much deeper than what you were feeling just five seconds ago. Your mind or cognitive state tells you that you're feeling one way, and your body tells you that you're feeling completely different, perhaps even completely opposite.

Scientists have told us that in the neurophysiologic feedback loops, these vibrations are invisible to the human eye. I demonstrate this with a **relaxation breathing technique** called 4–7–8. You start with a short exhale, then inhale for a count of 4, hold it for a count of 7, then exhale for a count of 8. You do this for a cycle of 3. So, you do: 4-7-8, 4-7-8, 4-7-8.

Whether you're sitting at home or driving, you can practice this relaxation technique. It makes your breathing become deeper and more regulated. With practice, you can take in more and more air, and your aim is to make it quieter and quieter. When I do this in my workshops, we practice this in two cycles of 4-7-8. After we finish, you could hear a pin drop on the floor. It inevitably becomes that quiet. Just two minutes earlier, the energy in the room was escalated. I was all fired up and lecturing with people sitting on the edge of their seats listening and writing notes. But the physiology of everyone in the group changes when we do the relaxation technique. Everything calms down. That's the power of our connection to one another physiologically.

What I often do in my lectures is give an example of a **negative feedback loop**. The dynamic is that we communicate in these feedback loops. You say one thing, I say another, you say one thing, I say another, and this little invisible feedback loop gets bigger and bigger and bigger. Before you know it, the loop has become all encompassing. That's why they say that laughter is contagious, because laughter is creating a **positive neurophysiologic feedback loop**. When there are two or three people laughing, and someone else comes up and says, "Hey, what's going on?", that person usually finds himself or herself laughing before even hearing the joke. That's the power of physiology; it pulls us in to other people. That's why people who are positive, energetic, uplifting, or passionate are so contagious and why we're drawn to them in the same way we're repelled by people who are negative and pessimistic.

The opposite of that laughter response is a **negative neurophysiologic feedback loop.** It's something you have experienced time and again from childhood to now. It's something you've experienced with your child on all levels. So, what I do in my sessions is have people practice a negative loop. I tell them that every time I say, "It's a great day," they're to say, "No, it's a terrible day." Many times, I unconsciously pick out someone who really has had a terrible day. It's the most fascinating thing that happens, even though I have no conscious intention of doing so. Again, it's the power of the unconscious. We instinctively know things that we don't know we know!

When I play that game with someone in my workshops, I have them answer me with "No, it's a terrible day" four times. Then, I ask them to answer my statement with "Yeah, you know, it really has been a great day." Whenever they make that positive statement, everyone in the room changes. I ask, "Did you feel that?" And everyone in the room says that when the participant made the "No, it's a terrible day" statement, they felt "intense," "anxious," "upset," "frustrated," or "fidgety." When the participant makes the positive statement, everyone says they feel relieved and calmer. It's that immediate and that powerful!

There has been **a study on parental depression** and the impact it has on infants by touch pioneer Tiffany Fields at the University of Miami. This is once again the power of negative neurophysiologic feedback loops. The harsh truth is that if you're depressed as a parent or if you're emotionally absent, what you communicate to your child on a physiologic level is stress and fear. The study examined a depressed couple with a baby and a healthy couple with a baby. The babies were hooked up to brain scans. When the healthy parent held her baby and then put it down, the baby's brain scan looked exactly the same as the other baby's brain scan when the depressed parent walked *toward* that baby. You know how a baby feels when its mother puts it down. Well, that is how the other baby felt when the depressed parent walked toward it. So, when the parent who is in a positive state puts down the baby and walks away, it triggers fear and stress in the baby because the parent is no longer there to protect it. When that parent walks away and doesn't acknowledge the baby's reaction, the parent is fostering the negative feedback loop. Stress will show up on that baby's monitor.

But when the depressed parent moves *toward* the baby, that depressed parent is communicating fear and stress to the child on a nonverbal level. Of course, the baby is supposed to feel safer and more secure when the parent approaches, but the parent's emotional state prevents the baby from experiencing what would naturally be a positive neurologic feedback loop. Again, that's the power of unconscious communication.

I want you to begin to pay close attention to the dynamic when you and your child get into an interaction that involves negative words thrown back and forth. Look at how big the dynamic becomes. Let me illustrate it through an exercise. Draw a small circle on a piece of paper right now. That's your child saying, "No, I'm not going to do it." Draw another little circle. That's you saying, "Yes, you are!" The child says, "No, I'm not!" Then, you say, "Yes you are!" Draw the circles larger around each time. That's the power of a negative feedback loop.

But positive neurophysiologic feedback loops are just as powerful. **A negative cellular state of communication cannot persist in the midst of a positive feedback loop.** Positive neurophysiologic feedback loops have the power to embrace negative feedback loops without letting the negativity escape in an eruption. It's like the positive loop suppresses the negativity. The negativity goes right into the middle of the circle, and the positive surrounds it.

So, when a child says, "No I'm not going to do it," the negative loop begins immediately. But when the parent takes a few deep breaths, and says, "I hear what you're saying," that parent immediately creates a positive feedback loop. It might play out like this: The child then says, "No matter what you say, I'm not going to do it!" The negativity goes right to the center. Then, the parent backs away and says, "I can tell that you're really scared right now. You must think something really bad is going to happen, or you must be really angry right now." This is a positive feedback loop. The child says, "Well, I'm still not going to do it." (Do you hear the subtle change?) The parent then says, "I know that you only want to be loved and that you feel afraid sometimes that I'm not going to love you. You feel afraid that you're not going to have a house here to live in." The child hears this, and a part of the child is frustrated because their negativity has to shut down slowly but surely. The parent says, "I know how scared you are right now, honey, and I just wish you would allow me to just love you and keep you safe because I'm not going to hurt you." All of a sudden, the child's eyes begin to well up with tears. The child's negativity gets stuck right in the middle, and the positive loop compresses right down on it.

The significance of this is that when one person is able to maintain his or her state of regulation, controlling the amygdala (fear center of the brain) it becomes very powerful—just like the laughter response or the way the room changes when someone acknowledges it's a great day as opposed to a lousy day. Signals are sent from the amygdala of the regulated person directly to the amygdala of the other person. The physiologic communication of the regulated person causes the dysregulated person to shift and become more regulated. The signals of the regulated person's amygdala embrace the scared, dysregulated amygdala of the other person.

LOVE AGAINST FEAR

Not long ago, a mother told me about a dynamic she was experiencing with her son. He had a trauma history and a very reactive amygdala. When he became scared, he went into survival mode, believing he had to fight for his life and that everyone would hurt him. They were in the garage after an especially stressful day, and her son was in a particularly amygdala-driven state. As far as he was concerned from this illogical state of being, his mother was out for his blood. She was actually standing still, but he came after her. She picked up a broomstick, put it between them, and said, "I know you're really angry right now, and I know you want to kill me."

This was a 9-year-old child. Can you sense the power here of his mother's presence? She was able to maintain regulation and accurately identify her son's emotional state. Mom was holding him at bay with the broomstick, but she remained regulated. A part of him wanted to go after her, but her statement caused him to say, "No I don't. I don't want to do that. I don't want to kill you. I don't even want to hurt you." Now, that's powerful! That is love against fear. This mother's brightness grew bigger and bigger until it encompassed the darkness of her son, making it impossible for him to *not* regulate.

If you have a negative feedback loop continuing with a child who is sensitive or has a history of trauma, the most effective way to challenge and confront that child's darkness is through your brightness. When you can create regulation within yourself in the midst of your child's dysregulation, you become the true essence of a parent — a positive influence on the growth and development of your child. But if your child sends negative signals to you, and you react by sending negative signals back, both of you will remain trapped in the darkness. In the neurophysiologic feedback loop, counter the negative with the positive, and the negative simply cannot grow. I know very well that it's a difficult thing to do, but it works.

The following three principles fit into the negative neurophysiologic feedback loop:

1. When we're in a place of stress, we can't help someone else through their stress. We act out negative behaviors in the midst of someone else's negative behaviors. We can't help them move into the positive if we remain in the negative.

2. When we're in a place of fear, we can't help someone else with their fear.

3. This is unconscious stuff, and as long as it remains unconscious, we're powerless to change it. You have to shine

the light of consciousness upon your unconscious state and admit to yourself, "I feel scared. I feel scared. I feel scared."

I have worked with parents whose lives have been consumed with fear, so I suggest that when they get up in the morning, the first thing they do is look in the mirror and say, "I feel scared" 20 times to themselves. This keeps that fear at a conscious level. Here's an example. A mother told me some of her history, and I said, "I see a lot of fear there." She said, "But I don't feel scared." So, I asked her to try the exercise in front of the mirror. Throughout the day, I asked her to continue to say it to herself, keeping that fear at a conscious level. She said, "Well, I'll try it but I don't really feel scared." The next week, she came back to me and said, "You know, I've been trying that 'I feel scared' thing that you told me to do. I think I've been scared my whole life." Is that not powerful? She brought her unconscious feelings into her conscious awareness.

Here's another example. A mother emailed me about her child's bath time problems. She said "Every night, I go into my child's bedroom and say, 'Okay, honey, it's time for a bath.' And she flips out on the floor, kicking and screaming, spitting, yelling, saying, 'I'm not going to do it. No way am I going to do it!' So, what I do is I jump on her and I do holding with her. I hold her for about 45 minutes until she calms down. So, we get up and go to the bathroom. As soon as she sees the bathtub, she is flipping out, kicking, and screaming all over again. This time, whether she likes it or not, I am getting in that tub with her, and she's going to take a bath. I'm going to wash her. I'm going to wash her hair. It's going to happen."

Can't you just see this scene? Water all over the place, and they both finally fall on the floor exhausted. Then, the mother says, "And she won't even go to sleep."

This mother had previously been through two years of attachment therapy with her child, and she knew her daughter had a trauma history. She knew her daughter wasn't relating to her in a very healthy way, but after two years of therapy, the therapist said, "You're cured." But the truth is that a "cure" isn't the point. **You** don't resolve—you integrate. The goal is integration, not resolution. It's about integration, education, and healing.

Any time there is any interaction between two people, those two people bring their physiology to that interaction. This is the power of being response-able. **Children with a trauma history are extremely sensitive.** Their physiological systems are extremely sensitive to the states of other people. As the adult, if you move into stress or some of your own unfinished business becomes activated, a sensitive child will react to you. If you're really stressed out—even if you just had a bad day and walk past this child—the child will react to you. This doesn't mean that you can never have a bad day. It simply means that it helps to stay aware that whenever you interact with another person, you bring all of your "stuff" to the table.

When we look at the bath time situation with the mother and daughter, it's evident that they're both bringing a lot of stuff to the table. **Any time you have severe behavior, you have a "trauma link."** In working with the mother and daughter, I needed to determine how much of the "stuff" belonged to the daughter and how much of it belonged to the mother. **If a parent can't calm down their own stress reaction, they can't calm their child's stress reaction.** Don't we so often say, *"Just calm down, calm down, calm down,"* in our frantic, anxiety-ridden state? **You can't calm someone else down when you're not calm yourself.**

Another important piece of information related to this story and many that will follow in this book is that **adopted and foster children usually exhibit severe behaviors around transition.** This is because one of their first transitions was traumatic—they never returned to their biological parent. One of their first transitions in their whole lives was a traumatic break, and, naturally, they had a grief reaction. Now, **any time they have to go through a transition, it re-triggers that same original transition trauma, complete with all of its emotions and fears.**

I emailed the mother, saying, "Here's what I want you to do. When your daughter starts flipping out on the bed or floor, I want you to sit on the bed, put your hand on your stomach and take some deep breaths. And I want you to ask yourself, 'how do I feel?' Then, after you have done that, I don't want you to do anything else with your daughter. I want you to email me back after you've done only that."

The mother emailed me and said, "That doesn't sound like very sound therapeutic advice." This mother happened to have been a marriage and family therapist herself for 30 years. She was a woman with a great deal of knowledge. So, I emailed her again and said, "Well, you asked me for the advice, so give it a shot. Try it out, and let me know."

The lesson of this is: Don't reject the knowledge immediately. Give the knowledge a chance to work in your life. If you don't give the knowledge a chance to work in your life, you'll never know what could happen. If all you're experiencing right now is negative, trying something different can only move you to a different place. So, don't reject the suggestion out of hand. The bottom line is: **If the child is not winning, the parent is not winning either.**

A couple of days later, this mother called me and said, "I tried out that technique that you prescribed. I had no belief that it was going to work and in fact it began just as I thought it would. I went in and mentioned that it's bath time, and my daughter immediately started flipping out on the floor, kicking and screaming—but this time, I went and sat down on the bed. I felt like a complete idiot—sitting down on the bed when my daughter is kicking and screaming, throwing a tantrum. Do you realize that in less than 10 seconds, she completely stopped what she was doing, climbed up on my lap as if she needed a hug, realized that she didn't, and then she went and took a bath? That was almost too much for me. I almost fell over."

That was the beginning of the end of their bath time problems. That's the power of bringing brightness immediately into the darkness and transforming a life with one experience, one occasion, one paradigm-shifting experience. Later, we discovered the trauma link that was working in this little girl's life. When she was picked up by Child Protective Services, she lived in a very neglectful environment. There were tons of lice on her head, and she was very dirty. Her first bath after that experience must be connected to tremendous trauma, so a simple bath took her back to this horrific part of her past. It's no different than a Vietnam veteran reacting to firecrackers because of post-traumatic stress disorder.

Another mother heard this story and said, "I had a similar situation with my own 10-year-old daughter. Every time I said 'shower,' she got really defiant, so I thought I would try your advice. I was very calm. I was breathing, and when I said it was time to take a shower, she immediately started to become defiant and telling me she didn't want to. I looked at her, and I was very calm. I said, 'Honey, if you need anything, I'll be right there. You just tell me.'" This mother said that her daughter literally went immediately into the bathroom and got in the shower. The mother was blown away—just completely shocked. She said that they had been battling with this problem for five years. She said, "My daughter got in the shower, and she did like she always does. She said, 'Mom, there's soap on the floor. I got water on me, Mom. The water's too hot. Now, it's too cold. Mom, there's water in my eyes.' She always did that, and I would get frustrated because I had to go back and forth. This time, I went in and was calm. I did what she needed. I said, 'Honey, I'm going to stay right here. If you need anything else, I'll be right here.' It went so well I couldn't believe it."

But this mother didn't stop there. She said, "I never considered that my daughter was afraid of something that had to do with the shower. So, when she got out of the shower, I said, 'Honey, come here and sit down beside me on the couch.' I put my arm around her and said, 'Honey, that shower went so well. That was the best one we've had in such a long time. Honey, what scares you about taking a shower?'" Her 10-year-old looked at her and said, "Mom, the guy who sexually abused me made me take a shower with him." WHAM! Talk about changing a paradigm with an emotional impact. Do you think this mother had a paradigm-shifting experience right there? In five years' time, they had experienced nightly arguments, fighting, defiance, stress, and fear. This child was terrified of taking a shower, and her mother didn't know it simply because she had never asked. She didn't know it because her paradigm hadn't challenged her to look underneath the behavior to something deeper. The paradigm had never asked her to look for fear. When she did, five years of difficulty were completely dissipated with one or two sentences.

The lesson of this is that **all severe behavior is almost always predictable.** It won't necessarily be predictable to the person who's acting out the behavior, but if you, as the parent, watch the severe behavior, you will begin to see that it's almost always connected to a specific place, time, situation, or person. This will give you an idea of what triggers your child's stress and fear.

What do you think this mother did next? She said to her daughter, "Honey, you don't have to take a shower anymore." The daughter started taking baths instead, and in no time, that mother emailed me and said, "You know what? She is taking a bath so fast sometimes that I don't even realize she's gotten in there and gotten out. I can't believe this." Six months later, the daughter began to take showers—all by herself. Can you see that what took place between this mother and daughter was a win-win?

Three-Phase Intervention

The **Three-Phase Intervention** consists of: **Reflect, Relate, and Regulate.** As long as your child is not at risk of hurting him or herself or someone else, the first thing you do as a parent is stop and reflect. You ask yourself, "How am *I* feeling right now!" Stop in your tracks and ask *yourself* because I don't believe it's okay for a parent to say to a child, "Tell me how you feel" unless the parent has examined his or her own feelings. When you connect to yourself, you can then communicate to your child in a secure way about what you're feeling. So, first, reflect on your own internal state, and do the 4-7-8 breathing technique to get in touch with your own fear. Breathe, calm yourself down, and embrace your fear, even if your child is having a tantrum at the same time.

Next, is the **Relate** phase of the intervention. While you're breathing and growing in your brightness, you say to your child, "I feel scared right now, and I need to know how you feel." In the midst of the tantrum, your child may say, "I don't know how I feel." Remember that **in the midst of stress, our thinking processes become confused and distorted, and our short-term memory is suppressed.** You were unable to determine how you felt until you stopped, took some breaths, and connected with yourself, right? The same is true of your child. So, you say again, "I feel scared right now. How do you feel?" Your child may again say, "I don't know." So, watch his behavior. If you see anger, identify it as such: "I think you're mad right now. You look mad to me. Are you feeling angry?" Your child then has permission to say, "I'm mad right now." And because you have calmed yourself down and are no longer threatened by your child's anger, you can say, "Give me more."

What happens in intense states of emotion is that all of the energy and vibration grows like a tornado or a hurricane. Because our society hasn't learned how to express emotions in a healthy and positive way, we act out our emotions in our behavior. We tear things up like the tornado. That's what kids do. **They become violent because they have no other means for expressing their fear.**

When you reflect your child's anger by saying, "You look angry," you can say, "I want your anger. I can see it. Give it to me." The anger may twist and scream, and it may kick and hit, but it will not be able to get outside of your positive feedback loop. It will be contained inside the positive loop. When you say, "Tell me, tell me louder, tell me more," you're encouraging the screaming and yelling. You're encouraging your child to use their words and emotions instead of their behavior.

If the child continues to hit, kick, and scream right in your face, you might find that it's too much for you to handle. So go slow, and be gentle with yourself. You might surprise yourself, however, and discover that when you come from a place of regulation, you're more comfortable with your child's extreme behavior than you thought you would be. **In our society, we're taught that behavioral acting out is okay and that emotional expression is not okay.** We tell kids not to cry, yell, or talk to us in an angry fashion. Then, they have no alternative but to redirect the energy into behavior. Those emotions have to go somewhere. So, I'm asking you to recondition yourself and go against the norm, helping your child to release those emotions directly.

This is why these techniques are so powerful because I'm going against the norm. God says that "Perfect love casts out all fear." Love encourages expression of emotion, while fear suppresses and runs from it.

It's very important, however, that you recognize that you respond differently to a child you think is angry and a child you believe is fearful. Right now, in your mind's eye, envision two children standing side by side. See an angry child and a scared child, and pay attention to your physiological reaction to each. Look at the angry child, and then, look at the scared child. Your body's state will change in reaction to each of these emotions. In order for you to respond proactively to a child you think is angry, you need to recognize that fear is under that anger. Remember that there are only two emotions: love and fear. You don't want the child's anger to trigger your own fear, which will only escalate the situation.

The third phase of the intervention is Regulate. I like to tell the story about the first time I met my now good friend Kathy Thorbjornsen. In the middle of a lecture in Norfolk, Virginia, Kathy stood up and said, "Dr. Post, I want to be one of the parents you talk about." Everyone in the room laughed, including me, and I said, "I want you to be one of the parents I talk about." This was an adoptive mother raising a very creative and talented daughter. She said, "I'm going to try this stuff, and I'll let you know how it worked."

That evening, I was giving a parenting class at the distinguished Children's Hospital of the Kings Daughters on the three-phase intervention, and guess who stood up? It was Kathy from my earlier lecture! She said, "I've got something to tell you. Today after school, I picked up my daughter, and it's always a bad day because she never wants to leave. She always gives me defiance and back talk. But this day, I walked in and was going to be calm. I got there early and was breathing, and I said, 'Honey, it's time to go.' And she started in with the same dynamics as usual, so I said, 'Mom feels scared right now.' My daughter stopped, looked at me, and said, 'Mom, what are you afraid of? Are you scared someone is going to hurt me? Are you scared someone is going to hurt you?' I said, 'No, honey. I'm scared because every day is like this, and the evening is like this. And we're not having a very good relationship.'" Her daughter looked at her and said, "Mom, everything's going to be okay." And they walked out of that school hand in hand. Kathy told me that before she came to my class, her daughter helped her set the dinner table. "We have had one of the best days that we have ever had," she told me. All of this happened as a result of: Reflect, Relate, and Regulate. Six years later Kathy's daughter has gone on to star in television commercials and shows!

TIME-IN

Time-in is essentially the opposite of time-out. The first truth to recognize is that **children don't act out *for* attention. Children act out because they *need* attention.** The time-out paradigm says, "Children act out *for* attention; therefore, you give them some time out to think about their behavior." The time-in paradigm says, "Children act out because they *need* attention." Therefore, you address this by bringing them close to you to regulate their fear and stress. What they need in those moments is not to put their nose in a corner. They need regulatory relating with you. You bring them in; you don't put them out.

When children act out, they're demonstrating that they've gone outside of their window of tolerance. Their stress and fear cannot be maintained any longer, and it explodes through that window of tolerance to a state of dysregulation, which causes the behavior. When your child is misbehaving, he is communicating to you in this way because he doesn't know how to communicate in words. He is essentially saying, "Mom, Mom, Mom, Dad, Dad, Dad, I don't know what to do right now. I need your help." *When this happens, the child needs time-in.* You do it for a 5-year-old, you do it for a 2-year-old, and you do it for an 18-year-old.

I have said to some parents, "Your child doesn't need to go to school tomorrow. He needs to spend the whole day with you." A mother and a 16-year-old spent the whole day together, and the mother emailed me to say, "I can't believe how powerful that was! It just reorients me to everything that I always knew—that I have to connect with my son in order for him to feel loved, because otherwise he doesn't feel it."

I created a challenge once to help families with severe behaviors. It was designed to help them within 30 days by receiving nothing more than a designed system of implementation and phone coaching. I actually gave them a guarantee that they would see a dramatic change. One of the participants was a very courageous mother. I asked her to try time-in. After she did, she called me and said, "I tried time-in the other day on my 7-year-old. I said, 'Honey, come over here and sit with me because I can see that you're really stressed out and scared right now. Why don't you come and sit by Mama? When you get ready, you can go back and play.' Usually, we do the time-out for seven minutes, but this time I did the time-in. Do you realize that my daughter sat beside me for 45 minutes? I absolutely could not believe that she sat beside me for 45 minutes."

Let your child decide how much time-in they need. You don't give them the minute-for-every-year formula. I don't know where that came from. But, when children are capable, let them decide. Try it with your child, and you may be surprised. On the other hand, if you say, "As soon as you feel safe, you can go back to play," and your child runs out to play within two minutes, you will need to make the decision for them. Decide on a timeframe based on how you assess the child's feelings.

Time-in says, "I can see that you're really scared. Come spend some time with me." The difference between time-in and a consequence is in the way it's communicated. It's in the way the physiology communicates. I don't advocate for the parent formulated consequences that most educators and counselors teach. And I also wish to make the point that there is a big difference between a parent formulated consequence and a natural consequence. Natural consequences occur naturally, thus being natural. You cannot control, prevent, or avoid them, they occur naturally. Natural consequences cannot be taught. For more on this I suggest getting *Beyond Consequences, Logic and Control* written by Heather Forbes and myself. I believe that most consequences are blame and fear-based, and do not teach responsibility but rather teach reactivity. Remember a consequence is a reaction to an action, so be mindful of what you think you may be teaching when using some of the common consequence based parenting models. Consequences don't encourage parents to take responsibility. They encourage parents to blame children for their behaviors because they come from that same paradigm that says children act out for attention.

When you use time-in as a consequence, it looks like this: The parent sees the child misbehave and says, "I can see that you don't want to play like everyone else right now because if you wanted to play, you wouldn't be out there fussing and kicking. So, get over here and have some time-in with me." That's time-in as a consequence. That's blame-based.

Time-in as a love-based intervention that creates regulation says, "Whoa! Come here. Hurry, hurry! Wow, I can see that you're stressed out right now and really scared. Why don't you hang out here with me for a little bit. When you start feeling a little safer, then you can go back out and play." There's a huge, huge difference in the resulting dynamic, but you can see that it's also a fine line in terms of how you word your response.

When you have a very sensitive child who is easily stressed and easily scared—especially those with traumatic histories—time-in is exactly what they need. Simply say, "Honey, come on over here and stay with me for a little while." "Stay here with me while I'm doing this or while I'm doing that." "Stay here on the couch with me and watch my show with me." "Sit here in the kitchen with me." "Sit here in the bathroom with me." "Sit over here on the park bench with me." You bring the child in because the child needs *your* attention. Some children will need a lot of your attention. So, if you have a child that needs a lot of your attention, what you want to practice is **containment**.

CONTAINMENT

Due to their sensitive or traumatic histories, some children are unable to be on the playground like everyone else. They're not able to be on the church grounds with everyone else sitting in the group because they might hit someone, hurt someone, or bite someone. The reason they do this is because it's simply too much stimulation, and they become dysregulated in this environment. The child is unconsciously saying, "I need containment."

Containment is like the foundation to time-in because the dynamic is that you're creating regulation between you and your child. You keep the child close to you in order to decrease the space that causes the child to feel threatened. This regulated interaction allows the child to calm down in an environment where he or she doesn't feel threatened. Containment is a dynamic that can be used in schools, with parents in the home, in markets, or in malls.

I work with a family that has seven adopted children. When they were planning a trip to Disney World, I asked them what they were going to do there with seven kids. The mother said, "I'm going to keep them close." I said, *"You better believe it!"* That's containment. When you keep them close, there is a greater likelihood for regulation because you are regulated, and they're feeling your regulation. When that happens, the whole environment changes.

I was once at a consultation in Canada at a residential treatment center. I took all of the kids to the park. (There were five or six of them.) All of them had an array of behaviors and diagnoses, including fetal alcohol syndrome, reactive attachment disorder, and opposition defiant disorder. They were all out there playing in the park, and I was working to create a big, nice regulated environment for them. But one of the little guys named Tyler started to get a little dysregulated, and he started to kick the sand. He said to me, "You know I don't like you. I hate you. You know you're a _____ this and a _____ that." So, I said "Hey, come here buddy." He came marching over. He was mad, and I said, "It looks like you're stressed out. Why don't you hang out here with me for a minute?" He said,

"I don't want to." So, I said, "I know you don't. I know you'd rather be out there playing, but right now, you're not in a very good place to be playing. You're really stressed out. I need to help you feel safe. Why don't you hang out here with me for a minute?" I knelt on the ground. I never even stood up. He hung out there with me for about five or ten minutes until I said, "All right, buddy, go ahead and go play." He was out playing for about five minutes before he started to dysregulate all over again. Who made the mistake? I did.

As the adult in the environment, I am the **significant regulatory figure**. I made the mistake because I wasn't attuned to myself or to him, and I let him go back before he was ready. Five minutes later, he was kicking and cursing all over again. I said, "Uh-oh, come back, buddy." I stood up this time. He was on the other side of the jungle gym and said, "I'm not going to. I don't want to do that anymore. That's stupid." So, he turned his back and acted like he was moving away from me.

When I first got to the residential center, one of the first things I had been told about Tyler was that he had a tendency to run away. So, he started to go, but he turned and looked back over his shoulder. I just stood there and took a couple of steps to the side, not toward him. He was a good 30 yards from me when I raised my hand and motioned for him to come back. Then, I looked away from him. He walked away, which only demonstrated how deeply dysregulated and scared he was. He was ready to fall back into his familiar state level behaviors of fight, flight, or freeze. His tendency, of course, was to flee. His state level told him that as soon as the threat became too big, it was time to get out of there.

Guess what I wasn't doing? I wasn't triggering him. I wasn't adding to the stress. I was letting my light shine, and my brightness was getting bigger and bigger and bigger. He wrestled with that. He wanted to take off running, but he kept looking back. His negative feedback couldn't grow. I compressed it because I refused to increase his stress. He finally started walking back toward me. As he headed in my direction, he cursed and said, "This is stupid" over and over. Then, he said, "I'm mad." So, I said, "That's okay. I can imagine that you are. I can tell that you're really mad. Hang out here with me." And we just sat there. Finally, it was time to go, and I said, "Guys, let's go." They all lined up, and I was still holding Tyler's hand. I said, "You know what, Tyler? I have to apologize to you." He said, "What for?" He wasn't cursing anymore. He was calm. I said, "Back there earlier, I let you go too quick. I should have kept you there a little bit longer with me. Then, I wouldn't have had to expose you to that stress all over again. I wouldn't have had to call you back to me." He looked at me and said, "That's okay, Bryan."

AFFECTION PRESCRIPTION 10-20-10

This is a prescription that I give to most all of the parents I work with. It consists of the following:

10 minutes of parent/child quality time in the morning

20 minutes of parent/child quality time after school

10 minutes of parent/child quality time in the evening

When you follow the 10-20-10 prescription, it quadruples the national average for parent-child interaction. That's how little time most parents spend with their children in the U.S.!

This prescription alone can have a significant impact on your child's window of tolerance and regulation abilities. You are creating containment on a regular basis and having proactive time-in with your child.

Put these ideas into action. Be powerful. Shine your light. Don't walk in darkness. Really make a change in your life, and it will create a change in your family's life and the life of your child.

————◆•▶◀•◆————

Chapter 2

LYING

Everyone tells white lies at times, but why do we do it? You guessed it: *stress*. This stress causes the brain to have a fear reaction, which leads us to protect ourselves by telling the lie. So, can you understand why a child with a trauma history might be prone to lying? The child isn't trying to be manipulative or defiant. The lying is a result of stress.

When a child lies repeatedly, it's a matter of utter dysregulation. In the distortion of the mind, the child believes survival is dependent upon convincing you that the lie is true. To this child, it's a matter of life and death.

I recall one instance where a mother and father came to me regarding their 14-year-old son. "He lies all the time about nothing at all," his mother told me. "He lies about going to school, going to wrestling. It doesn't matter what the situation is—he lies about it."

When I questioned these parents, I learned that their son had indeed experienced trauma in his past. It was obvious that their son was reacting from stress. As a result of his lying, however, the parents had told their son, "If you don't stop lying, you're going to boot camp." Wouldn't you feel stressed if someone threatened to abandon you? Obviously, saying something like this to their son only escalated matters because it sent him into an even more severe state of dysregulation. I cannot emphasize this enough: ***Never* tell a** child—especially a foster or adopted child—that they won't have a place to live if they don't stop their behavior. Presenting a child with such consequences will absolutely defeat your purposes. In fact, presenting your child with any kind of consequences while he is in a state of dysregulation is pointless.

Remember the **two things that happen with stress:**

1. The normal thinking process becomes confused and distorted, and
2. Short-term memory is suppressed.

In the moment of confrontation, giving a child consequences will add more stress, which leads to more confusion, distortion, and suppression of short-term memory. This means that the child won't even remember the consequences the next time he lies. It's not that the child is refusing to remember; it's that dysregulation *prevents* the child from remembering.

THE FORMULA

I instructed these parents to try three steps consistently for two weeks, after which I asked them to call me. Rather than calling me in two weeks, however, they called me six weeks later. They had implemented the three steps of the formula for that period of time, and their son had made a complete turnaround. The boy had even secured a job. This is only one example of the success of the formula. In fact, in some cases, these steps have been effective after a single use.

Here are the steps:

1. Make sure your child is going to school every single day. If he/she isn't showing up for class, it's a safety issue, and **nothing else matters if there's a safety issue.** First and foremost, the child must be kept physically safe. How can you accomplish this? You must call the school, email the teacher, and even go to the school, if necessary, to make sure your child is there. Do whatever it takes to ensure that your child is in school and out of harm's way.
2. Every night—without exception—turn off the television, put

down the newspaper, and give your child 20 minutes of your undivided attention. Resist the urge to lecture, and allow your child to talk about anything he wants—that's right: *anything*. If your child doesn't want to talk and remains silent, simply stay there and be present with the child. Even if you're both quiet for 20 minutes, you're still putting in the time with your child.

3. When you know for certain that your child has told you a lie, **ignore the lie, but don't ignore the child.** I know this can be difficult for parents, but remember that when your child is lying, he is in a state of dysregulation. Until your child has re-regulated, you can't reason with him and will only add to his stress if you attempt to talk about the lie. So, ignore the lie at first, but don't ignore the child. Instead, give your child a hug, and tell him you love him. Reassure him that everything is going to be okay and that you're not going anywhere. Spend 5–10 minutes with your child offering this reassurance. This will help your child to re-regulate from the stressful reaction that resulted in the lie.

    After this time with your child, address your own dysregulation by going somewhere alone and dealing with your own stress. You might feel angry or frightened about your child's lie. Calm yourself down, and after an hour or two, come back to your child and address him from your heart. At that time, say, "Son, when you tell me a lie, it really hurts me." Don't insist that your child tell you the truth. This will only result in another lie.

Depending upon the child, you may have to apply this formula several times, but the results are powerful. In some instances, just the undivided attention for 20 minutes per day is enough to shift the behavior.

Unfinished Business

Are you finding it difficult to think about ignoring your child's lie? I recall one mother's reaction. It was a definitive and immediate emotional response: "I can't do that!" So, I asked her, "Who lied to you?"

She responded that her father had lied to her all the time. "It used to make me so upset," she said. "There's no way that I'm going to ignore my child lying now. I can't do it!"

The problem is that parents go into their own state of dysregulation when a child lies. The lie causes a threat reaction in our brains, and we enter our own hyper-aroused stress state. Saying, "Tell me the truth!" triggers additional stress in the child, and when both parent and child are triggered into survival, it's like pouring fuel on a flame. Like the mother mentioned above, this emotional reactivity is a result of unfinished business from the past. She responded to her child's lie so strongly because it triggered emotions from her experiences with her father that she had not yet fully processed.

Once she had made the connection between her reaction to her child's lie and her father's lying in her own childhood, however, she was able to compose herself enough to ignore her child's lie. After trying the formula for a short period of time, her child's lies stopped.

When you ignore your child's lie, your own amygdala doesn't become triggered. You are then able to remain calmer yourself, as well as create a safer physiological environment for your child.

This formula gives both you and your child the time you need to re-regulate from the stress that is the root cause of the lies. Only then can your child's behavior change.

—◆•◗◆◖•◆—

Chapter 3

TRANSITION ISSUES

This is one of the most common issues that I encounter while consulting with schools and parents concerning challenging children. If you're able to make positive changes in the home, those changes will naturally translate into the school environment. As you learned in the introductory chapters, difficulties with transition have to do with stress. Children with trauma histories, particularly those who have been adopted or put into foster care, have enormous stress and trauma related to transition. That first transition of being removed from the biological parent was enormous. Every time the child is faced with a transition, the response is fear that he'll experience the same pain that he experienced during that first transition. The child isn't consciously aware that he's experiencing fear. His amygdala is activated, and he's in survival mode. All he knows is that he must protect himself or die. It's that dramatic.

Transition is one of the most difficult areas that children struggle with, and they immediately revert to their fear barrier. So, your 12-year-old may revert to the age of 3 during transitions. For instance, I was consulting with a mother recently who told me she's having difficulties with her adolescent son. She was aware that she was being triggered herself because of her own trauma history. Naturally, any stress that her son acted out would create regression in her.

When she regresses to her own adolescence, she can only react to her son from that emotional age. Remember: **when we encounter a novel event, we perceive that event as a threat until deemed otherwise.** What that means is that anytime we encounter something new or are encouraged to do something new, we perceive it as a threat until we can prove it to be safe. It takes most of us a millisecond to shift from that place to the next. That is a transition. Children with trauma histories have had brain impacts that prevent them from making this shift so quickly.

I was giving a lecture to a group of parents and professionals, and I said, "Let me know if there's anything you want me to go over." One mother said, "Yeah, there is something I want you to go over. I have a son who poops in his pants all the time, non-stop, for six years." I said "Tell me about his history." The mother said, "We adopted him when he was four. He basically went back and forth between us and his mother, but we have him now. He's a good kid, but he just poops his pants all the time." I told her that it sounded like trauma and stress—that he's afraid of something. The mother said she didn't understand. So, I asked her to tell me why she thinks her son was repeatedly pooping in his pants. She said, "He does it because he's trying to control us. He poops his pants because he's saying, 'Poop on you, Mom and Dad.' He's doing it because he's angry." I told her I had heard that paradigm explanation before. So, I simply said to her, "Okay, well, maybe something will come up in the lecture today that will help with this." I continued with my talk and later came back to this mother and said, "Here's the deal. If you're willing to work with me on this for two weeks, I will guarantee a 50% reduction in your son's behavior, if not a total elimination of the problem, because I'm on to what this child is doing." The mother said, "Well, it's probably pretty expensive." I said, "I'll do it for free." She said, "You're telling me he can't control it, that he's not doing it for control, and that he does it because he's scared? Well, I'm not buying it."

I was flabbergasted. "After we spent a whole six hours and one day going through all of these details with lots of examples, you're still not buying it?" So, I walked up close to her and slammed my hand down on the table beside us. WHAM! What did she do? She jumped. I said "Did you see that?" And I did it again. I then said, "What I want you to do is to control that response. Don't jump this time." WHAM! She jumped again. "Control it!" I said. WHAM! Finally, she said, "Okay, I get it! I get it!"

Remember the two things I told you it takes to **shift a paradigm? Repetition and emotional impact**. This woman was getting it intellectually but wasn't shifting her emotional paradigm. For this woman's son, the first four years of his life were filled with chaos and terror. He was moved back and forth between her family and his biological mother, never knowing where he'd be or if he'd have a home. Think about how traumatic that must have been? Yet, we underplay this and discount its significance.

I told her, "Your son has trauma around transition. When he experiences any transition, his amygdala gets triggered. It sends a signal to his gut, which makes him do what? It makes him poop in his pants. He poops in his pants just because the bell rings. When the bell rings, it's a transition. He can be in the living room with his friends, and one of them might say, 'Let's go outside,' and he poops in his pants." She said, "Absolutely. We can't even go out to eat. We're driving along and we can't even say, 'We're going to a restaurant to eat' because he'll poop in his pants."

Traditional attachment therapy says, "You need to make him wear his dirty pants and stay in the car because nobody likes a smelly child. He needs to learn. That way, he won't poop in his pants just before you go into the restaurant and try to control everybody else." Do you hear the distinction between the power of the two paradigms? Do you hear the distinction when I say "He's scared, and he's pooping in his pants because of the transition?" Transition for him is attached to trauma. Remember: **If the child is not winning, the parent is not winning either.**

The other aspect of this boy's development is that he was never fully potty trained. His body/mind system never even made the connection: bowels full=go to restroom for release; bladder's full=go to restroom for release.

Dealing With Transitions

1. Before a transition, say to the child, "Honey, I know you're terrified any time you have to go somewhere. When you have to do something different, even going up to your room, you're terrified. It all relates to back when you were a little boy, you went between our home, which was secure and loving, and your mother's home. Your mother was addicted to drugs and in and out of jail. The transition was terrifying for you all the time, so now your body (touch your finger to your stomach and heart) communicates to your brain (touch your head) that there's something really, really scary about changes. But you're not aware that you're feeling this, so we're going to work on it and help you realize your fear."

   That's shining the light of consciousness on the unconscious. When you shine the light of consciousness on the unconscious, the unconscious is unable to continue to have so much control. When you talk to your child about transitioning, talk to him about his unconscious fear. You need to be able to open this up for him so that he can understand it better. Then, you need to practice **positive repetitious conditioning** with transitions.

2. Go to the child, and wrap your arms around him. Then say, "Honey, tell me right now that you feel scared." Put your hands on either side of his face, and say, "Tell me right now, 'I feel scared.' Now take some deep breaths, and let's go to the car. Take deep breaths, say 'I feel scared,' and keep taking deep breaths. Remember that you get scared when you go to the car, and when you get scared, you poop in your pants. Now, tell me when you're scared, even if you don't know for sure that you're scared. Just say you're getting scared. When your body is feeling scared, the more you get used to it, and the more you start prac-

ticing it, you'll know more often when you're feeling scared. It's when you don't know that you're feeling scared that you poop in your pants."

3. I can guarantee that while he's doing this process with you, he won't poop in his pants. You can then go for a drive and ask him to keep saying, "I feel scared." When you get to the restaurant, you can say, "Keep breathing. We're going to go into the restaurant." Rub his shoulders and say, "We're going to have some ice cream. Keep breathing, honey, and keep saying 'I feel scared'." This is interrupting the transition and creating positive repetitious conditioning.

TRANSITIONS IN SCHOOL

When this happens in school, it's best if the teacher agrees to go to the child and put her hand on his shoulder before the bell rings. She can discreetly say, "Okay, Jonathan, the bell's going to be ringing in about 20 seconds. See the clock? Start breathing, because you know you get really scared sometimes when the bell rings. You sit here until everyone gets up and leaves. Focus on your fear. When the bell rings, I will walk you to class." Through this process, you bring consciousness to the unconscious.

I don't think I have ever worked with a child with a trauma history who didn't have some problems in school. If your child has difficulties in school, try these techniques for the next 14 to 30 days. I will guarantee dramatic improvement if you change just these three areas, keeping in consideration the transitions involved.

These three areas are: **group activities, cafeteria, and recess.** The most significant thing going on in these environments is an increase in sensory stimulation. **An increase in sensory stimulation is equivalent to an increased threat.** When the child perceives threat and moves into fear and stress, he's not thinking about finishing that group project, eating his food, or winning the game. He's thinking about surviving in the environment.

As a result of this stress, Sara ends up getting stabbed with the scissors, Tommy gets his milk knocked over and poked with a fork, and Jane gets kicked on the playground. So, what do you do? With communication, expression, processing, and understanding, you can bring the light of consciousness to the unconscious.

Even 4-year-olds can get this information. I worked with a 4-year-old who was struggling in the classroom, and his mother happened to be a teacher in a classroom on the other side of the hall. He was struggling with the three areas even though his mother was just across the hall. Yet, when she was finally able to help him communicate, express, process, and understand how he became scared in each of the three environments, guess what he did one day when it was time to go to the cafeteria? He walked to his mother's classroom, and with big eyes, he said, "Mommy, I don't want to go down there." Prior to this time, he would have simply become defiant. His mother would have said, "Go down there and eat. You have to eat." This would have culminated in a tantrum. But because of understanding, his mother said (without becoming reactive), "Sam, what's wrong?" He responded, "It's scary down there, Mom." Immediately, the light bulb went on, and she said, "Well, you just come and sit down with me, and I'll walk down there with you as soon as I finish up what I'm doing."

What negative repetitious conditions have you set up when your child reacts with fear in these environments? Recognize these conditions, and begin to create containment and positive repetitious conditions.

Containment decreases the threatening space, essentially reducing the sensory stimulation, and reducing the child's stress in the environment. Without containment, the child will move into dysregulation and survival mode.

Teacher Instructions

Hopefully, your child's teacher will be open to receiving these instructions to help your child stay more regulated during school-time transitions.

GROUP ACTIVITIES

A child who struggles in group activities acts out at their emotional age, not their chronological age. You can be sure that regression is taking place in this situation. When you have a child who is regressing to these emotional states, you need to assess them to determine their emotional age. If the child is 13 but has an emotional age of 4, you can only have expectations of that child based on the age of 4 when that child is in stress. So, instead of putting this child into a group of five, reduce that specific child's group to three children, and see how that works. When you reduce the group to three, put the child in a group with two of the brightest children, and tell them they all have to work together and help one another out. Give them permission to help one another.

Next, stay closer to that child, and become more aware. Go back every few minutes, and ask the group, "Are you doing okay?" Every time you check in, you're **prolonging the child's regulation**. You're creating more security and containment.

CAFETERIA

For a child with cafeteria-related stress, have the child walk behind you and stay close to you, or let someone else in the class lead the group while you walk in the back of the line with the child. As your class goes through the cafeteria line, stay with the child. Don't walk off and sit at your own table. Stay with the child.

Next, have a specific place for this child to sit, preferably one that is close to the teacher's table. Remember that this is containment, not punishment. It's about keeping the child safe **proactively, not reactively** where you end up kicking the child out of school. Many schools have a problem with shifting out of the reactive paradigm to the proactive paradigm. When they shift out of the reactive to the proactive, great things begin happening for these children.

Recess

Containment is especially important during recess. Remember to communicate to the child, "We know that these events are very stimulating and scary for you." Then, get the child out of class before everyone else, and take him to the playground. Say to him, "We know you really want to play with everyone else, and this is not a punishment. But we know you really struggle when everyone else is out here playing, so this is your area right here." Then, mark it off for him. "This is the area where we can keep you safe. If you get out of this area, we cannot help you to feel safe. If you go out of this area and you get angry or upset and end up getting in trouble, we can't keep you safe that way. That's why we need to keep you here in this space." When the child comes out, you or the playground monitor stands close to the vortex at the top of the space—the top corner. The significance is that the monitor is closer to him, thus creating more safety and security for him in that space.

If there is no monitor, or the school cannot provide a contained environment, don't send the child out to recess. Let him spend time with someone he trusts and feels safe with, perhaps the janitor, a coach, or in the secretary's office. Create a dynamic where he doesn't have to be out on the playground without supervised containment. Remember that we're shifting the paradigm from reactive to proactive. When you create containment, you keep the child safe and reduce the stimulation that causes the threat. You want to prolong the period of time that the child feels safe in the environment.

If you do these things when the child experiences these difficult transitions, I guarantee that you'll experience a dramatic improvement in the child's behavior.

Chapter 4

STEALING AND SELF-MUTILATION

Why are stealing and self-mutilation lumped together in the same chapter? You might be surprised to learn that both are **addictive behaviors**. Stealing and self-mutilation are no different from addictions to coffee, caffeine, chocolate, shopping, gambling, pornography, alcohol, or drugs. The higher the state of dysregulation, the more severe the habit becomes. This is because **addiction is an external attempt to soothe an internal state**. In other words, it's an effort to regulate.

Even small children become involved in addictive behaviors, and as they get older, they succumb to more severe addictions. For example, marijuana is the gateway for other drugs for many people. As they get older, the soothing impact of the original substance no longer has the same effect, so they must seek something stronger to reach that soothed internal state.

STEALING

I used to steal a lot when I was younger. I know now that it was a byproduct of my own dysregulation. I would steal anything. It didn't matter what it was. It was a physiological payoff for that moment, but 5 or 10 minutes later, the rush wore off, and more stress set in as the worry about getting caught only added to my state of dysregulation.

Children with traumatic stress histories steal to try to ease their internal state of dysregulation. It's the same as with any addictive behavior. As soon as children take something that doesn't belong to them, they get an enormous chemical reaction—a rush or release. This reaction varies from person to person. For example, boys tend toward a hyper-aroused state, which is similar to the rush that comes from cocaine—a stimulant. In girls, the reaction is more likely to be a hypo-aroused state which is more like the release that comes from heroin—a suppressant.

As children repeat the addictive behavior, their systems become conditioned to that behavior. Such a child then believes that all he needs to do is put that object in his pocket in order for everything to be okay—at least for those 5 minutes. When the dysregulation returns a few minutes later, the child may steal again and again.

Children also steal in **specific environments** as a reaction to **certain events.** A child who steals from the teacher's desk, for example, is likely to steal from that teacher's desk more than any other place in the classroom because of conditioning. A child may steal in a store because he's triggered from the stress of going from the car to the store, or it may be a result of overwhelming stimulation in the store environment. Parents are usually unaware that something as innocuous as going to a store can be enormously stressful for a child, particularly a child with a trauma background. Think of it for a moment. For example, if a child were passed from one foster family to another before being adopted, any kind of change in environment might trigger dysregulation.

A 17-year-old girl once said to me, "I'm terrified going into stores. I feel like I'm going to walk into the store and knock over something, and everyone is going to stare at me." That is a powerful piece of relationship-transforming information.

If your child developed the habit of stealing in an effort to re-regulate, there are steps you can take that are very effective in helping the child stop the addictive behavior.

THE FORMULA TO END STEALING

Here are the steps to help your child stop stealing:

1. First, you must make sure that you are in a calm state yourself. Then, from a very non-blaming place, say to your child: "When you get stressed out, you have a tendency to put things in your pocket that don't belong to you, and the reason you do that is because it makes you feel good. So, come to me when you're stressed out or scared. When you put things in your pocket that don't belong to you, it hurts other people, and that might lead them to get angry with you. But I need you to understand that **I know** when you steal it's because you're scared or stressed out. So, when we go to the store, I'm going to keep you close by me."

   The teacher who understands this formula might say to a student who is prone to stealing, "Ben, you know I'm not going to let you be by yourself. I'm going to bring you with me." If the teacher must leave without the child, give him a hug, and tell him, "It's going to be all right, and if you get scared, wait for me out in the hall."

   This process creates a **container** for the child, helping to alleviate the feelings of threat that cause the stealing behavior. Instead of becoming soothed by the rush or release of stealing, your child is soothed by your non-blaming presence. In this way, you also lessen the sensory input that can be overwhelming in a store environment. Keeping the child close to you helps the child to feel safe, and this reduces the incidence of stealing — not because you're watching, but because you're creating a state of regulation for your child.

2. Practice going to the store or wherever the child is prone to stealing. Remember that we regress when we're stressed, so a child who steals is regressing to a younger age in those moments. Tell your child that you will hold her hand at first. Holding your child's hand can help create a state of regulation. That skin

to skin contact is very comforting, and I have found that even teenagers are often willing to do this. When a parent offers a hand, the child *unconsciously* feels safer.

The next week, your child will stand near you. Later, you will be no more than five feet away. In this way, you are building up your child's ability to tolerate these environments and lessen the stress. Of course, if any of these steps prove to be too much for your child at any time, stop and go back to the previous step. Don't rush the process. If holding hands is too stressful, going into the store may be too stressful just yet. Remain as patient as necessary.

If your child is old enough, you can ask how she's feeling as you're taking steps toward the store. Focus less on the behavior of stealing and more on the emotions that are leading to the behavior. This will help you get to the root cause of the stress.

At first, practice going to the store without shopping. You don't have to buy anything. Hold the child's hand from the car to the store, walk down the aisle, and walk back out. Then, try it in another day or so. Gradually, you can work up to spending more time in the store.

In my experience, when your child experiences regulation in a situation where dysregulation is common, the body/mind system can develop rapidly. In 14 to 30 days, there can be a 50% reduction in stealing behavior, if not a total elimination of it.

SELF-MUTILATION

Self-mutilation is a very appalling behavior which, understandably, frightens parents a great deal. But just like stealing, it's an **addictive** behavior. Again, it's an external attempt to soothe an internal state. **Children communicate through their behavior,** so a child who cuts herself is communicating that she wants you to attend to her. She just doesn't know how to ask.

The majority of people who self-mutilate are adolescent girls who have been diagnosed with borderline personality disorder. When borderline personality disorder is involved, you can be certain that there is a history of trauma. In self-mutilation cases, the child is usually going into a deep state of hypo-arousal. The child might say, "I cut myself in order to feel. I feel numb. Cutting feels good." I have also heard: "I cut myself because it excites me" and "I cut myself because that's the only way I can get out of my skin."

Obviously, it's difficult for parents to handle their own state of dysregulation in the face of something so dramatic. But as you have already learned, "freaking out" about behavior that is caused by stress in the first place will only cause more stress. You must put your own fear and anger aside in order to address the problem. Only then can you help your child move from dysregulation to re-regulation. Your child needs you to calm your own state of stress so that you can be there for her and help her to feel calm.

THE FORMULA TO END SELF-MUTILATION

1. **Explaining is empowering**, so explain to your child why she is cutting herself. We have to explain the process of healing if we truly want to empower someone to heal. Say to your child, "You cut yourself because you become stressed, and your body shuts you down, making you feel numb. Cutting yourself feels good because you no longer feel numb. In fact, if you didn't think it hurt so much, you'd probably bang your head against the concrete. It's that intense. So, let's think about where this comes from. Maybe I can help you figure out the emotions that trigger this. Do you think it's because of rejection? Abandonment? Physical abuse? Divorce? Sexual abuse? Did you witness a traumatic event? Talk to me so that I can understand and help you understand even better."

   Take your child in your arms and say, "Tell me what's going on in your life. Talk to me." Then, you have to make it okay for your child to tell you anything without losing your composure about it. For those moments, hear everything calmly. If there are issues to be dealt with, do it later. For now, create that container for your child to feel safe talking to you.

2. Tell your child, "The next time you feel the need to cut, come to me. Let's just sit with each other for a few minutes instead. We can talk, or we can just sit quietly. We can hold hands if you like. Whatever you want. But I want you to come to me first. Then, if you still feel the need to cut yourself, you can go do that."

    I know that's a very difficult thing to say to your child, but the truth is that you won't be able to prevent your child from cutting. And it may take several attempts before the formula works, but eventually, the child is almost certain to stop needing to cut because you're alleviating the stress by creating that safe container. You are creating a safe alternative that will provide the soothing effect instead of the cutting.

In one case, a mother and daughter simply spent 20 minutes together daily. This was scary at first because they had not been spending anything other than superficial time together. I instructed the mother to go to her daughter's room and just sit with her if the daughter didn't want to talk. The 18-year-old ranted and raved, telling her mother to get out. So, the mother waited outside her daughter's room for three days straight — 20 minutes each time. The teenager told her mother how stupid she was for sitting there every day. But on the fourth day, the teenager said, "Fine! Come in here and sit down." This led to a little bit of conversation, and gradually, they became more open with one another until the behavior changed. The mother's persistence paid off, and it eventually created a safe container for her daughter to share with the mother. Once the teenager understood that her mother wasn't going to "freak out" anymore, they could work together to create a state of re-regulation that eliminated the need for the addictive behavior.

Chapter 5

AGGRESSION, DEFIANCE, AND CHORES

How are aggression, defiance, and chores related? All three of these behavior problems relate to your child regressing to his emotional age rather than his chronological age. Something is causing the child to go into stress, and when that happens, your 13-year-old may regress to the age of 6.

AGGRESSION

A mother who tried one of my techniques came to me to say it wasn't working. Her son had been aggressive with her, so I advised her to give him space and refuse to engage in the conflict. He was unwilling to let her do that, however. When she walked away during his outbursts, he followed her or became aggressive with her younger children in order to keep her in the conflict.

In this case, her child was desperate for regulation. He followed her in an effort to get out of the intense stress he was feeling. He didn't have the capability for getting out of the situation in any other way or expressing his true needs.

So, I suggested to this mother that she walk with her son into another room and sit with him. Then, she could say, "Son, you have my full and undivided attention." I asked her to place her hands down in a non-threatening position and say, "I can tell you're very angry right now. You're needing something, and I don't know what you're needing, which makes me feel helpless." Then, I suggested she encourage him to tell her what he thought he needed and felt in that moment.

When parents encourage their children to let out the anger, even if it means screaming at the top of their lungs, the stress is greatly relieved. When the child does that, he redirects all of those feelings. It becomes verbal, which is where you want his feelings to go. When he's able to verbalize his anger, it will cease to be acted out in an aggressive or violent way.

Whenever the child becomes aggressive, practice this process with him. You might say, "When you're feeling stressed and scared, I know you're feeling that way because you're following me around and don't listen to anything I say. Let's practice now and every other day to talk about what you need and feel." This creates positive repetitious conditioning.

If you can implement these principles for two weeks, you will see a significant change in your child's behavior. If you continue on within 30-60 days, you will be amazed at what you see in relation to their behavior.

What exactly is going on when a child becomes aggressive? Remember the discussion of the amygdala. When we experience **trauma** or traumatic stress, it impacts our brain in the little **fear receptor** called the **amygdala**. When we experience stress, that fear receptor becomes **hypersensitive** to threat. The amygdala is **reactive** based on stimulation to our **sensory pathways** primarily through what we smell, what we see, through body language, through temperature, and through touch. All of those things directly trigger the amygdala. A lot of times the amygdala can be triggered by more than just words. Physiological research tells us that 90% of communication is **nonverbal**. When a child becomes aggressive, it's a child who is prone to a **hyper-aroused** state. Remember that the amygdala is responsible for three reactions: **Fight, flight, or freeze.** The immediate reaction that we all have to a new event or novel stimulus is to *freeze*. Dr. Bruce Perry says that **in times of encountering a novel event or stimulant, we all perceive that event as a threat until deemed otherwise.**

Aggressive children start primarily in a place of freeze, and from that place of freeze, they move into their preferred state of **hypo or hyper-arousal.** Boys tend to move into hyper-arousal, so they have a tendency to be more aggressive, while girls have a tendency to move into hypo-arousal and become depressed. You will find, though, that children with traumatic stress histories can vacillate between the two states. The common denominator, however, is that the freeze reaction is the first reaction. The aggressive child's amygdala has been supercharged. Dr. Bruce Perry calls this state in children an "**amygdala hijacking.**" He says that their amygdalas hijack their brains.

A great example is a group of children who know each other and are playing in the backyard. All of a sudden Benji gets tripped. Benji has been playing, and **peer physiology is equal to stress physiology,** so Benji's amygdala goes into a hyper-aroused state. He may hit the ground and freeze initially, but he then melts into the hyper-aroused state. At that point, Benji moves into a state of dysregulation, a state outside of his window of tolerance. In this state, Benji begins to seek out threat. He becomes vigilant to threat. Then, what happens? The next little boy who comes running past him gets it right in the nose.

I have heard of situations and seen situations where kids who grew up in orphanages from a very young age all the way up to 8-10 years of age exhibit a tendency to get into fights when they're in groups with other kids. And it becomes apparent that the child who was assaulted didn't really do anything to provoke the attack. So, aggressive children move immediately from a place of freeze to a place of hyper-arousal. They immediately move into a place of **defense.** This reaction is **the essence of fear.** We're not aggressive out of spite, meanness, or hate, even though that's the way it may appear. We become aggressive out of a **survival** state. When that amygdala is triggered, especially with children who have a trauma history, it triggers the survival state level.

It gets even more dynamic than that because literally, at the cellular level for this child, in that state of stress, *their cells constrict into survival mode.* Take both of your arms right now, and wrap them around you. Try to experience that you are in a place of absolute terror. That is the experience of the aggressive child in the hyper-aroused state. Now, imagine if someone approaches you while you're in that state. Remember that we perceive novel events as threats until deemed otherwise. If you're in a state of absolute terror, and someone approaches you, your immediate reaction is that this person is a threat. If your hyper-aroused state then brings up all of the traumatic stress that you've experienced, there isn't much likelihood that you'll be able to melt and become flexible enough within milliseconds to determine this person approaching you *isn't* a threat.

As adults, we have a greater capacity for our upper level thinking processes (the hippocampus) to kick in quickly and override the assessment of our amygdalas. But children with traumatic stress histories don't have the same capacity. Because of their traumatic stress experiences, their thinking processes will literally become **overwhelmed.** That's what stress does to our thinking. We become confused and distorted. So, in that distortion, a woman who is actually 5 feet tall can suddenly become 6 feet tall to a child and become a gargantuan threat. In the child's psyche, there is no alternative but to attack.

Aggressive Toddlers

Think about how these scenarios play out for this aggressive child day by day from toddler to teenager. You take the toddler to an early school program at 3 years old, he starts biting everyone. The toddler moved from a place of relative safety within the home into a place of high stimulation. It may seem to you that you're putting your 3-year-old into a seemingly non-threatening situation, but look at it from the perspective of the child. There are bright lights, lots of noise, and both adult and child strangers. See the bombardment of the child's sensory system? They don't even have to have a history of traumatic stress to react in this way. This response can be caused by the mere fact that he's a toddler whose full regulatory developmental capacities haven't kicked in yet.

Remember that the hippocampus does not complete its development until the 36th month of life, so the toddler may not have all of that available to him yet. Let's say the child has an early history of traumatic stress. When all of that stimulation comes toward him, the only thing he knows to do for his survival is move into an aggressive state. As soon as another child moves toward him, he bites the other child. The teacher then picks up the biting child and gets bitten herself. The child doesn't have the facility to react in any other way.

So, what do you do with a toddler who is biting or hitting other kids at preschool? Rather than have the child go immediately into a group activity, leave the child at the start of the school day with a specific teacher or aide. He or she stays with that teacher for a short time. This child may need more time than the other kids to regulate before going into a group activity.

If you start from the very beginning to **contain** this regulated environment through this relationship with the teacher, the child might not go into hyper-arousal. As the day continues, you can let the child have a bit more space. But when he's out playing with the other kids, don't just leave him there and look at him like he's just one of the other children. Stay aware of his tendency to become more stressed, more afraid, and, therefore, aggressive. Pay more attention to him, and keep an eye on him when his face starts to become red or his hands go on the hip. That's when it's time to say, "Tommy, come and stand over here by me."

AGGRESSIVE TEENAGERS

How does this play out in a teenager? Let's say the teenager comes home after a very stressful day at school. It was a day of trying to maintain his own sense of regulation so that he wouldn't hurt someone when he felt threatened—which is pretty much all of the time. Let's say he was able to maintain regulation, and he gets home after a hard, stressful day which included football practice with a coach on his case, poor nutrition, and having to sit in a chair all day long. He comes home and is really stressed out. As soon as he walks in the door, his father jumps on his case about something that happened the night before. That teenage boy is in hypo-arousal before he even gets home. As soon as his father gets on his case, he'll move right into either hyper-arousal or deeper into hypo-arousal. A lot of times you see this with teenagers. They struggle between the hypo and the hyper-arousal states. The hypo-aroused state is one of withdrawal, depression, resistance, and/or defiance. So, when Dad jumps on the teen's case, the kid says, "I don't want to talk about it. Get out of my face!" What happens next? Dad gets triggered!

As soon as Dad gets triggered, his physiology communicates stress and fear. Then, the teen moves into hyper-arousal or a deeper state of hypo-arousal. If, in his own stress, the father says, "Don't you talk to me like that!", the son will walk into his room or wheel on his father in anger, saying, "I'll talk to you any way I want to." From that point, you have two threatened beings going after one another, both in survival mode. This gets them nowhere except perhaps a fight. It's a negative neurophysiologic loop.

It isn't that the son or the father aggressively attack one another. It's that they're in **mutual states of stress**. The father needs to understand that any time he sees his child, especially his teenager, in a place of hypo- or hyper-arousal, he will experience an immediate trigger of stress himself, which will create a fear reaction.

Stress and fear reactivity lead us to the need to control the environment. There are many professionals who say parents have to be in control, but I'm telling you that establishing control out of stress and fear reactivity will get you into trouble with your hyper- or hypo-aroused child. The truth is that **the only time we seek to control is**

when we are afraid. The only time we seek to control is when we're in a place of stress. When we're regulated, we don't seek to control.

If the father can begin to pick up on his son's signals to realize that the teen is in an aroused state, then the father can begin to notice his own reactions. He can say to himself, "My son is really stressed out right now, and that triggers something in me." The father also needs to understand that when his son comes home from the school environment, it's not the best time to address his teenager. So, when his son comes in the door, Dad takes a deep breath, and lets his son go right into his room. Dad follows him into his room and sits on the bed. They don't have to say anything at that point. Remember that the aim is to create a relationship that will allow regulation to seep in without pouring fuel on the flame of dysregulation and aggression. So, Dad says, "Son, I'll bet you had a tough day today." Dad can only do this when he is in touch with his own fear reaction. His son may say, "You're sure right about that. I had a tough day. That coach is a real son of a gun." Dad can then say, "I remember when I used to play football how terrible I used to feel about that sometimes. What did the coach make you do today?"

All of a sudden, the father is relating to his son's feelings. "Tell me about how that made you feel? That must have made you feel terrible." He continues to process with his son, but he's only able to do that because he recognized and connected with his own fear trigger. Once they have communication going, and Dad starts to sense that his son is starting to regulate, he can end the conversation. He leaves and comes back a little bit later, saying, "You know, son, last night, we didn't have such a good evening, you and I. I was feeling pretty stressed out, and I'll bet you were probably feeling the same. What can we do to have a better time tonight?" The communication changes when we're not in a place of stress. If we don't see the fear underneath the anger, we only see the aggression. But remember that the emotion underlying the anger and aggressive behavior is fear.

With aggressive children, first and foremost, you have to see

that the aggression is not directed toward you. The aggression is directed toward survival. I encourage parents to go into another room and close the door when their children move into a hyper-aroused state. In some cases, children can't determine whether or not you're a threat, even if you're not approaching them. So, even if you're just sitting there, a raised eyebrow can be enough of a trigger to send some children into aggression. If the parents leave the room entirely, there can be no resistance because the child has nothing to resist against.

When a child is in an aggressive state, the child is seeking regulation, but if the child has experienced a lot of trauma, he or she may not be able to accept the regulation. Not only can they not regulate themselves, they cannot allow other people to create the regulation for them. In that capacity, you have to give the child some space to allow some of that higher, upper level hippocampus thinking to kick in. So, move away if you must. Allow the child to follow you because even in the act of following you, the child begins to perceive that you are not a threat. The more you can stay back, the more the child will start to regulate and lock into that higher level thinking to see that you're indeed not a threat.

Defiance

Aggression and defiance are very similar. A defiant child is reacting the same as an aggressive child, perceiving an event as a threat until deemed otherwise. A defiant child is a scared child, and that child moves into a state of hypo-arousal. It doesn't make any difference if this child is defiant toward going to the bathroom, brushing their teeth, taking out the trash, getting in the car, going to class, putting on their tee shirt, or going to bed. Fundamentally, this child is scared, perhaps even terrified, depending upon their history. As soon as you make a request of the child, the request is perceived as a threat. They immediately go into freeze mode, then into a hypo-aroused state, and the result is defiance.

In the moment that your child becomes defiant, she actually can't perceive whether your request is safe or a threat. Remember that everything is perceived as a threat *until* it is deemed as safe. So, in the moment, your child is defiant.

If you have an adopted or foster child, you'll probably experience a lot of defiance around the **issue of transition**. Remember when we discussed those first awful transitions that such children go through? It doesn't matter the age when this traumatic transition occurred. From that time forward, the child could have a negative association with any transition of any nature, and this will be a fundamental dynamic for defiance.

As soon as you say, "Hey, Johnny, let's go to McDonald's," Johnny doesn't run and get into the car like his brothers and sisters. He stands there and says, "No, I don't want to go." Or he may start looking for his shoes and walking in circles. As soon as he finds his shoes, he has to go to the bathroom, where he locks himself in. Of course, everyone else begins to feel frustrated, which is just another type of fear. So, what do they say? "Johnny, hurry up!" And how do you think that makes Johnny feel? Even more stressed! How do you address the situation when Johnny avoids leaving for school every single morning?

I consulted with a school once about a child who was failing terribly in all of his classes. I asked about his history and was told that he recently lost a parent. You know what that told me? Something about school was terrifying that child. This child was probably frightened that he might go home from school to find he had no parent left. Does that make sense to you? I suggested they **allow the child to call home twice during the day**. Do you know what happened to his grades? Everyone was blown away because his grades immediately started to improve. He felt free to go to school. He didn't delay in the mornings anymore. He stopped being depressed about going to school. He had been terrified that at the end of the day, he would not have a parent at home, and the calls alleviated his fears.

So, how do you deal with Johnny every time you come to a transition? Try this out right away. Sit down with Johnny, pull him onto your lap, and say, "Son, come here. You know, every time we get ready to go somewhere, you get really scared. And when you get scared, it triggers a lot of very old memories for you. You know what? When you were a very little boy before we adopted you, you lived with your biological mom for a very long time, and someone came and took you away from her. You know the reasons for that. Well, when they came and took you away, you never returned to her, and what happened is that when it's time to go somewhere, you remember that time and worry that something really scary is going to happen. So, anytime we get ready to go in the car, it makes you scared. How does that make you feel to hear that?" He might say, "I don't know," or he may say, "It makes me scared right now." Then, say to him, "Son, we're going to go get in the car right now, and we're going to go for a drive. Tell me how that feels for you. Do you feel something in your body somewhere? Tell me how scared that makes you." Get him to say it.

What you are doing is **communicating to his unconscious state** of being. You're encouraging him to **take that unconscious fear and make it conscious**. When you can communicate to Johnny what's going on, you give him control over that state. When he says, "Mom, I feel scared," you can put your arms around him and say, "Honey, everything's going to be okay. You're going to be with me, and I promise you we're going to come back home. I'm going to keep you safe." Practice this tonight, and see what happens. Of course, if it seems too much for him to go into the car the first night, don't force it. Try it again the next night.

The essence of defiance is fear. So, **give the child some space to perceive that the threat is not a threat but that it is safe.** You make your request and back away. What you have to realize is that this is a traumatic stress issue. You can't force the child to do what you want. If you do, you're just creating **negative repetitious conditions**. So, every time that you even mention that activity in the future, you'll get a stress reaction. Not only that, but it's going to cause a stress reaction in you just thinking about it. You have to see the child's fear, and you have to see your own trigger reaction as well.

DEFIANCE IN THE MORNING

If it's morning, wake your child up slowly and spend maybe 10 minutes sitting beside her. Don't wait until it's 10 minutes before school starts to say, "Hey, Susie, get up! Hurry! We're late for school!" You'll immediately send her into a hyper-aroused state. What's the child going to do? She's going to pull the covers right over her head. And if she gets up, she's going to go to school, acting hyperactive and defiant. You must wake her up slowly, giving her time to transition, and say, "Susie, I hope you slept well. It's time to wake up. We're going to have some breakfast. Take your time." Interact with her for 10 minutes until you know she's starting to wake up.

What does trauma do? It impacts the **circadian rhythms,** which means it's going to impact the way this child wakes up in the morning and calms down at night. Spend that 10 minutes, then turn on the light and say, "Rise and shine!" Then go. My mother used to do this. She flipped the light on, said, "Rise and shine," and walked away. She didn't say, "Rise and shine. Come on, it's time to get up. We're running late. You've got to get going!" By doing this, she allowed our circadian rhythms an opportunity to kick in. Then after about 5 minutes, she came back in and said, "Hey, sleepy head. It's time to get up."

Practice this ahead of time with the child. You can say, "Honey, we're going to practice what we're going to start doing in the morning. I want you to go lie down for 5 minutes and act like you're sleeping. Then, I'm going to come wake you up like it's morning. I know that you get really angry in the morning, so if we practice this tonight, we can work on you not being so angry in the mornings." When you start to practice this, it becomes a **positive repetitious condition.**

Defiance About Homework

A parent said to me, "I have a 14-year-old son who is terrified of school work. He was shutting down in school. I'm home schooling him now. I don't know how to handle his immediate reaction just at doing school work."

Does this sound familiar? It isn't an uncommon scenario. So, what's going on with your child? It has to do with the expectations he believes others have of him regarding homework. He probably believes he has to do it good enough or perfect in order to be loved. When I questioned the parent quoted above about her son, she mentioned that his learning disability causes him to become panicky when he has to work on a subject he finds difficult.

What I tell parents first of all is that a situation like this requires structure. If the child experiences stress related to school work, the anxiety will be triggered the minute you mention it. One way to offset this stress is to mention the homework the night before. You might say, "Tomorrow morning at 10:00, we have to do math, and at 1:00, we have to do reading. And I know that really scares you." When the child is expecting the structure of the homework and knows it's coming, he has time to calm down a bit.

So, the trick is to help your child become more conscious of the emotions going on inside. By acknowledging that he's scared, the cat is out of the bag, so to speak. Tell him that you realize he becomes panicky when it's time to do math or English because he has trouble with these subjects. Tell him: "I expect you to do it horribly. In fact, the worse it looks, the happier I'm going to be!"

No, you're not encouraging your child to fail. You're opening up a new way for him to *think* about homework, which opens up a new way for him to *execute* his homework. Up until now, he has thought, "No matter how I do it, it's not going to meet your expectations." When you relax your expectations, he's suddenly free to let go of the stress and find out exactly how well he can do. If you have your own perfectionist tendencies, you will need to deal with your own stress.

Allow your child to do it wrong. Ironically, this opens the door for him to do it right.

DEFIANCE AT HOME

Let's address one more scenario. Let's talk about defiance in the home with 8-year-old children. Remember that they tend to move back and forth between hypo- and hyper-arousal. Just because a child is in a home doesn't mean that they feel safe. Suppose you have an 8-year-old child watching T.V., and it's time for dinner. When you say it's time to turn off the T.V., you escalate the hyper-arousal state that he's already experiencing. Yes, just watching the T.V. causes him to act out!

What you have to do is allow time for the child to move out of that state of perceiving something as a threat until deemed otherwise. You must allow for more time between turning off the T.V. and coming to the dinner table. A child who becomes difficult when it's time for dinner is struggling with the transition. For this child, you want to go in 10- 15 minutes early and sit on the couch with her. You want to put your arm around her and watch T.V. with her. Physiologically, you have engaged her. In about 10 minutes, you can say, "Honey, in about 5 minutes, it will be time to turn off the T.V. and eat, okay?" She's going to say, "Oh, yeah, yeah, yeah" and will continue watching T.V. The significance is that she did hear you and is slowly but surely processing what will happen in 5 minutes. The little connections in her brain are starting to fire. Then, in about 10 minutes, you say, "It's time to turn the T.V. off." You can even say, "You can do it, or I can do it if it's too hard for you." Acknowledge the child's state. Or you could say, "Go ahead and turn the T.V. off. I know you get really scared, but come on in and help me with this. I could really use your help."

You might even say, "I know you get really scared when it's time to turn off the T.V. because you think that we'll never turn it on again." I know that sounds like a ridiculous fear. Your child is afraid you'll never turn on the T.V. again? Remember that your child's reality is not logical, and stress brings confusion and distortion.

The best thing to do is practice this first. Let the child watch T.V., and practice it before you have dinner. Just practice turning off the T.V. without having to go to dinner. This is **positive repetitious conditioning** that allows your child's body/mind system to become conditioned to turning that T.V. off one time.

CHORES

Difficulty with chores, of course, is a form of defiance. Let's say you have a child who's starting to get older, and it's time for her to take some responsibility in the house with a few chores. You list the chores that you learned how to do when you were a kid growing up. Your mother and father may have put the list on the refrigerator along with the time each needed to be done on a little calendar. Perhaps Saturday was your day off if you didn't have to pick up the leaves.

When you try the exact same thing with your child, the first time a chore is due to be done, what happens? Your child goes into a defiant hypo-aroused state. If you try to get the child to do the chore, you're met with aggression. And this dynamic plays out over and over again.

When you look at children performing chores, you're observing a developmental picture as much as a psychological or physiological picture. Remember that in times of stress, we revert back to our fear barrier. Children will immediately perceive the request to do a chore as overwhelming. In that state of overwhelm, they perceive the request as a threat. So, of course, the result is defiance. This response is especially true of children with any kind of trauma in their history.

These stress responses of overwhelm and threat cause the child to revert to her fear barrier, which essentially says, "No matter what I do, I can't accomplish this task."

One mother was aghast that she couldn't get her 8-year-old to do something as simple as make the bed, but the chore itself was not the issue. For the child, it evoked stress.

Take a moment to assess your child's emotional age in a time of stress. Where is your child emotionally when in stress? If your child is 12, does your child act like a 12-year-old when in stress? It's highly unlikely. We are all a product of chronological age, emotional age, and cognitive age, and these ages are rarely equivalent. It's more likely that your child is chronologically 12 and reverts to an emotional age of 2 or 4 or 5 when experiencing stress.

You need to have an idea of the child's emotional age when in stress. For example, if your daughter is 8, and her chore is to wash the car every Saturday, you chose that chore based on her chronological age. But your expectation can only be congruent with her emotional age, not her chronological age. Therefore, if you conclude that your child's emotional age is 4 (no matter the chronological age), you can only ask for chores that a 4-year-old could accomplish. A 4-year-old isn't capable of washing the car.

So, the first question you must ask yourself is, "Are my expectations for chores in line with my child's emotional age?"

But this is just the first piece of the puzzle. The child may still go into overwhelm and threat when asked to do chores. So, the next question to ask yourself is, "What is my reaction when my child becomes defiant?" Chances are, you move into stress as well. When that happens, you move out of a place of regulation, which also moves you out of a place of understanding. From that place, you can't begin to comprehend the overwhelming negative messages that a child receives when you "simply" say, "Turn off the television, go upstairs, and make your bed."

Number 1: Think about the T.V. going off and possibly never coming on again. Number two: Think about the transition of moving away from the T.V. to turning around to getting ready to go upstairs. Number 3: Think about the fear of what may happen during that transition of going upstairs from downstairs. Number 4: Think about the prospect of moving into the upstairs room, looking at the bed, and having the thought, "What if I don't make up this bed to Mom's expectations? What might happen then?"

If you have a foster child, that child's immediate thoughts would probably be: "If I don't make up the bed, I won't have a home. She won't love me or want me. She'll kick me out of the house. I'm going to have to pack my bags, and then, where am I going to go live?" I know how illogical that sounds to an adult, but when you're talking about fear barriers and stress, all of these thoughts become reality in a child's mind in a matter of milliseconds.

So, what do you do to alleviate the stress for both of you? One of the ways you can begin to stop this cycle is to eliminate some of the transitions involved. Look at all of the changes and transitions that occur with the chore. In our example, the 8-year-old must turn off the television, walk upstairs, go into the room, and make the bed. Eliminating some of the transitions would involve asking the child to make the bed *before* she comes downstairs and turns on the television.

Don't forget, however, that if this 8-year-old is reverting to the emotional age of 4, it may be too much to expect of her in that stress state to make up the bed at all. Did you expect her at the age of 4 to be able to make up the bed? When she's in stress, she may as well be chronologically 4 years old.

This is where teaching your child *regulatory interaction* is the key. Here's what you might say, "Honey, come with me, and let's go make your bed." Then, you begin by making the bed together.

If the chore is cleaning the floor, for example, you might say, "Honey, come up with me, and let's clean the floor." Then, you clean the floor together. If cleaning the entire floor is too much for the child the first day, you work only on one square area to start. You can say, "Don't worry about anything else but this square area today. Tomorrow, we'll work on keeping this square area clean, and then, we'll work on another square area, okay?"

While you do this, you create **positive repetitious conditioning**. You create positive associations with these activities. So, the next day, when you tell the child to take out the trash, you go with him to the back step, and he dumps it in. The day after that, you say, "I need you to take out the trash," and wait to see what happens. If he gets up and takes out the trash, it's time for a celebration. If he doesn't, he's communicating that he still needs your help. Continue helping with the chores until he starts to engage in it on his own.

If you've tried the traditional methods of rewards and punishment, you already know that they don't work. That's because these methods involve negative repetitious conditioning, and since your child is in stress, no reward or punishment is ever going to work. So, first, you have to alleviate the child's stress around the chore. Then, as the child starts to become more effective with the chores, you can begin offering rewards like allowance or ice cream.

———◆◦◆◦◆———

Chapter 6

MEALTIME, HOARDING, AND GORGING

Wᵉ know that mealtime, especially family time, is one of the most important regular events for the healthy development of children. In fact, research says that children who have meals with their family are, on average, more intelligent than children who don't. So, it's very important. But the bug in the ointment is that mealtime is also one of the most stressful scenarios in a family's day-to-day relating. It's a double-edged sword.

So, let's break down mealtime, hoarding, and gorging behaviors. For example, when your child wakes up in the middle of the night and goes to the cupboard to steal all that sugar, just sucking it down, down, down, remember that this is a stress reaction. It's *not* a consciously driven act. Your child doesn't wake up with the conscious thought, "I'm going to go and get this sugar to make someone else mad at me. I'm going to get this sugar because I'm really hungry and that's what sounds good to me. I'm going to get this sugar because I know I'm not supposed to have it."

No, this behavior is much deeper in the unconscious than that. When this child wakes up, the unconscious state is already in full and active mode, and it's driving the negative behavior. **Children with food-related issues *generally* have trauma related to food in their history.**

HOARDING

Hoarding of food is a behavior that has to be addressed systematically. You have to get away from the punitive and shame-based approaches. You have to get away from the approaches that deny children food. When a child hoards food, this is a child who, very early, probably formed stress around not having enough food to satisfy their hunger. Not only that, but this child probably had no one to feed and nurture her, giving the child more if needed or taking the food away if she was full. Many of these children didn't have that very important interaction in their first years of life.

Remember that there is negative repetitious conditioning and positive repetitious conditioning. We are a habitual species. In the case of this child, a lot of negative repetitious conditioning occurred around hunger. There was never a normal positive conditioned experience that involved crying followed by being fed. So, a child who has learned that soothing does not occur in relationship with other adults may learn that soothing occurs in relationship to food. Hoarding food is actually very addictive in nature, and an **addiction is an external attempt to soothe an internal state.**

Trauma as it relates to food impacts the brain in such a way that it actually causes the child to have a great deal of conflict within the internal system. The part of the brain that is impacted by this kind of trauma is called the suprachiasmatic nucleus (SCN.) The SCN sits right inside the hypothalamus gland and is a little bundle of nerves that's responsible for our circadian rhythms, which are intimately connected to our digestive processes, hunger pangs, and feelings of fullness. Our circadian rhythms are also connected to our ability to calm down, wake up, have meals, use the bathroom, and regulate our body temperature.

As you know by now, stress leads us to a state of hypo- or hyperarousal. If you take that a step further, in relation to stress, what are the two things we all do around food when we're stressed out? We either **overeat** or **under-eat.** A child with a trauma history will have a tendency to do both of those things to a greater degree. They're going to have a stronger tendency to really overeat, or they're going to have a stronger tendency to really under-eat. So, when it comes to hoarding, your child may react in different ways from day to day. You may have a child who hoards food not only in her bedroom, but overeats at any time that she's allowed to eat, or the child may shut down and refuse to eat at all when it's dinnertime. Then, in the middle of the night, she's up hoarding food.

A child who hoards food has come to rely on food as her sole source of regulation. Traditional parenting literature suggests giving such children some kind of consequence or providing behavior modification. But when you only give the child a consequence or create a behavior modification schedule, you fail to address the fear and stress that underlies the behavior.

1. Communicate to this child first of all, "Honey, I know that when you get stressed out, the first thing you want to do is eat. And more than anything, you probably want to eat sweet food because sweet food really helps you calm down." Tell the child the story of neglect if that's what's in her history. Once you've communicated to this child that you now understand that her hoarding behavior comes from a deeper place, communicate that it's important when she's stressed out or scared to come to you and tell you.

2. When the child is hungry, she comes to you. You say to this child, "When you get up in the middle of the night, come and wake me up. If you wake up, and you're stressed or scared, I want to know." That way, the child starts seeking *you* for regulation rather than food, even if that means you lose a little sleep in the process. When the child awakens you, spend a little time with her. Maybe go back to her bedroom with her, and soothe her back to sleep. If that doesn't work, and she still wants a snack, give it to her. I recommend that you feed the child the snack and even join her in eating something. And that snack doesn't always have to be a vegetable. How many of us seek

out vegetables when we're stressed out? We want something sweet because sweet foods are naturally occurring *attachment foods*. Sweet foods initiate the natural attachment hormones to allow us to begin to regulate in some subtle way and make small changes in our regulatory system. The significance, however, is that this regulatory result of the sweets doesn't last. They help us only in the moment.

3. Throughout the day, make sure the child gets plenty of snacks, leaving a basket of things that she can eat at any point during the day. I encourage foods like granola bars and bananas, which have a lot of natural sugar in them. This way, the child can eat something sweet but healthy whenever she becomes over-whelmed and stressed. You don't have to lock the refrigerator or the cupboards. When we lock the kitchen or the cupboard or lock the child in her room, we inadvertently resemble the orphanage experience that caused the trauma in the first place. There are lots of things we do that may feel natural but which actually create an environment similar to the neglectful environment the child came from. You need to create a safe environment.

4. In some situations, it's even helpful to give the child a bottle again because the child may have never received that kind of nurturing, which included being rocked and making eye contact with a loving adult. I've recommended that for 2-year-olds all the way up to 15-year-olds. The child must be in the parent's arms for this to work. It doesn't work if the child walks around with the bottle. If a child needs it, regardless of the age, they will take it. If they don't need it, they won't take it. And if they need it at first, they'll stop when they no longer need it. So, if you offer it, you'll know from the child's reaction if he or she needs it or not. It may be difficult for parents to imagine actually feeding a bottle to a 12-year-old, but the reality is if this child didn't get this necessary experience early in life, the child has a barrier in their development. Until that barrier is addressed, the other levels are going to continue to stagger.

5. Let's say you've tried the technique, but you happen to be cleaning your child's room and find 20 candy wrappers under the bed. What do you do? At this point, it's obviously too late. She didn't come to you. She didn't trust enough that you could create the relationship she needed to regulate. So, use those 20 wrappers as a sign that your child is, in fact, facing stress greater than she can handle. Then, you say, "Honey, I can tell that you've been really stressed out." She'll say, "How do you know that?" You tell her it's because you saw 20 wrappers under her bed and you know that the only time she hoards food is when she's stressed or feeling like no one is listening to her.

    Instead of being reactive, you're being responsive. So, use those setbacks as opportunities for further growth with your child. Now, you have an opportunity to communicate with her. That's the process of helping your child slowly and systematically overcome hoarding behaviors.

Remember that if you pay attention, you can usually predict severe negative behaviors. If you watch closely enough, you'll see that the child is hoarding that food in relation to **specific environments and specific settings**. The hoarding takes place at night, at school, during physical education class, or when in other people's houses. Those are signs that those environments are really over-stimulating and stressful for the child. This is when you need to create **containment** for the child to help her feel safe in those threatening environments. As long as she feels unsafe in those environments, she will seek the food to regulate. This is the child who looks for everyone's sweets in the cafeteria, is willing to trade all of her food, or gives all of her money or pencils for someone else's dessert.

GORGING

Gorging is another behavior demonstrated by children with trauma history around food. First of all, gorging also arises from a state of stress. Second of all, it arises from an emotion of fear that *there's not going to be enough food left over*. If a child is gorging, that child is almost certainly hoarding food as well. Third of all, just like hoarding and other behaviors, gorging is unconsciously driven.

It's similar to the normal behavior of a toddler who has been given a sweet treat. If you put a plate full of cookies in front of him, in many instances he will eat and eat and eat until the food is spilling out of his mouth. They won't stop until you intervene. So, gorging is very regressed behavior. The significance is that coming to sit at the dinner table is very stressful, and it naturally triggers the child back into some old **state level memories** where the trauma is buried. When this child sits down to eat, the state level is triggered, and he immediately starts reacting as though there's not going to be enough food. More than likely, there's been a tremendous amount of negative repetitious conditioning around mealtime where the child heard time and time again, "Slow down. Don't eat so fast. Don't talk with your mouth full. There's going to be more food. Stop acting like a pig. You're eating like a hog. Gosh, you're messy." Mealtime in and of itself became a very stressful event.

1. To relieve the child's stress during mealtime, have the child sit closer to you. When you start to observe the gorging, say nothing. Just slide your hand under the table, and pat the child on the knee. That will create some interruption to his natural state of stress. Something as simple as that can bring the child back into the present and allow him to slow down.

2. If that's not effective, you might want to offer to actually feed this child at the dinner table. In my experience, some children have been able to thrive by having a parent willing to feed them again for a short period of time. With small children, I encourage the parents to put the child in their lap and feed them. Again, this is a child who relies on food as the source of regulation rather than relationship as the source of regulation. So, create an environment where you begin regulating him and teaching him self-regulation.

3. Remember that a gorging child is a stressed child. Asking the

child to leave the table only adds to that stress. Just sitting at the table may be stressful for the child, so have him come inside 20 minutes ahead of mealtime and help you set the table or sit with you while you make dinner. This gives the child's circadian rhythms time to catch up and regulate before the meal experience. This also gives the child the chance to discover he's hungry, and if he eats at mealtime, he may not feel the need to hoard food in the middle of the night.

4. Another exercise is to have the child leave a bite or two of food on the plate at the end of the meal. That, in itself, can be profound because what the child experiences, both consciously and unconsciously, is that there's always going to be food. Cleaning his plate leaves an unconscious perception that there's not going to be any more food. The child has the perception that there isn't going to be any more food *ever*. Yes, this is an irrational response, but remember that stress and trauma cause confusion and distortion.

   That's why the child wakes up in the middle of the night in a stressed, scared state and thinks, "There's no food, there's no food, there's no food." That's what leads to the hoarding or gorging behavior. The child has to come to trust that the relationship with the parent can be a source of regulation instead of the food.

5. One question you might have is, "What if I'm sitting by my child with my hand on his knee, and even though I offer to feed him, he doesn't want me to touch him and continues to gorge?" What I want you to keep in mind is that sometimes, just sitting down at the dinner table can be overwhelming for a child. So, ahead of time, go to the child, sit down with him for 10 minutes, and say, "I know sitting down to dinner can be very stressful. I want you to know if it gets to be too much for you, we can always just get up and eat dinner together later." Give your child the option of not having to force himself through the stress in the moment.

Again, if you try these techniques, creating positive repetitious conditioning around mealtimes, you will quickly begin to see results. Your child will begin to regulate, and these behaviors will diminish.

Chapter 7

BEDTIME, BATH TIME, AND
BRUSHING TEETH

When someone says "Hey, how are you doing this morning?", the conscious processing part of the brain generally gives an automatic answer: "I'm doing fine." But in order to tap into the unconscious and offer a true depiction of how you're really feeling, you have to take a moment and ask yourself, "How am I doing right now?" You then stop and listen to that voice that says, "I'm not doing so well." That's the voice that says, "I'm worried about someone who has been sick in my family" or "I'm worried about paying the bills." Again, children don't act out in a negative way from a conscious place. It comes from an unconscious place.

As I talk about bedtime, bath time, and brushing teeth, think about the way the Stress Model fits into these behaviors. When your child struggles with these behaviors, he is acting out a state of neuro-physiologic (body/mind) stress. Between the stress and the behavior is a primary emotion, and since there are only two emotions, you know that it's fear. That emotion continually drives the behavior. If you can help the child recognize and express that emotion, process it, and understand it, you will calm the stress and diminish the behavior.

Remember that the underlying emotion is fear, no matter whether the behavior surfaces as defiance, manipulation, resistance, or aggression. A child in a place of love may initially resist going to bed, but that child will be able to regulate and relax enough to fall asleep. A child who can't relax enough to fall asleep is in a state of dysregulation and is trying to communicate this to you through her behavior because she isn't conscious enough about her emotions to verbalize to you exactly what's happening within her.

BEDTIME

Mealtime and bedtime have a common denominator: **circadian rhythms**. Circadian Rhythms are essentially the tiny little bundle of nerve fibers in the **hypothalamus** gland in the brain which sits right above the fear receptor, the **amygdala**. As you learned in the introductory chapters, the amygdala is what controls our ability to perceive fear and threat. These nerve fibers which dictate our circadian rhythms control our ability to start our intestinal system to grind up food. They encourage our autonomic response system to slow down and relax around bedtime. They encourage the nervous system to activate and get started in the morning.

So, why do I bring this up? **Trauma impacts the circadian rhythms.** Now you know that this is why your child with a trauma history has trouble with sleep. That's why your child with a trauma history gets up in the middle of the night and runs all over the place. That's why your child with a trauma history always sleeps best with you. These children exhibit significantly disrupted circadian rhythms, so that when night time comes, their rhythms cannot allow them to settle down and relax like everyone else.

There's another level that occurs in this situation. In their frustration and fatigue with a child who won't go to sleep, parents say, "You get in that bed and stay in your bed, or we're going to lock you in your room because we can't have you running all over the house. If you run out of bed, we're going to spank you!" As a result, the child is a product of that **negative repetitious conditioning** which means that night time automatically triggers **hyper-arousal**. In other words, in this way, parents inadvertently make it worse. Just mentioning that it's time for bed or just the fact that the sun starts to go down can send the child into a **fear reaction**.

One of my clients is a single parent with a 6-year-old who struggles with bedtime. The little girl was adopted when she was 2-3 months old. Her biological mother was very young and dysregulated, and she delivered the child during the heat of a Louisiana summer. The adoptive mother started the bedtime process at 7:30 p.m. in an effort to get her daughter to sleep by 9:00 p.m. This struggle went on for quite awhile. Mom became exhausted.

So, we began by giving the child space at night time. Mom continued the same routine, but now, she says, "It's time for Mommy to get some rest, but you stay up as long as you need to." When I suggest this, parents immediately worry that their child will stay up all night, but in my experience, this isn't what happens. That's because as soon as the mother says that Mommy needs some rest, there is no more threat of **negative repetitious conditioning**. There's no more wrestling and fighting over going to sleep. Immediately, there's a reduction in threat, which brings about a reduction in stress.

So, the mother would lie down on the bed, and the child played for another half hour. Remember that this is a 6-year-old who doesn't have the capacity to stay up all night. It's not about the child wanting to stay up all night. It's about the child being able to regulate in a timely manner around bedtime. The mother told her daughter, "When you get ready to lie down, come and get me, and I'll lie down with you." Any time the amygdala is triggered, the circadian rhythms will go out of whack. So, when the parent removes that threat, the child can regulate a little bit and settle down for the night.

For two nights in a row, this was very effective, but on the third night, the child acted out her fear when the mother said, "I'm going to lie down." The child hung onto her mother and threw things at her. What was the child trying to communicate in this very regressed place? It becomes so obvious when you look at it from the new paradigm. She was trying to communicate that she was really scared and didn't know what to do. All she knew was that she didn't want her mother to leave. She wasn't able to communicate this verbally, but her mother was able to "hear" it through her daughter's behavior. So, her mother said to her daughter, "Oh, I can hear you must be really scared right now even though you're not saying it. The only reason you would throw things at me is because you're scared and don't know how to communicate it." That opened up a huge dynamic between this mother and little girl, and they are now on their way to having an effective bedtime routine for the first time.

A lot of children are highly threatened around bedtime, so just the thought of going to bed triggers them. As a parent, you have to regulate yourself enough to give the child some space. If you have a consistent difficult bedtime scenario, begin practicing these techniques *tonight*.

Create a new routine. Start by saying, "We're going to start turning the T.V. off at 8:00. Then, you'll have from 8:00-8:30 to do whatever you need to do. Then, we're going to read a story. At 9:00, I'm going to go to my bedroom, and you can stay up in your room as long as you want. I know when it comes time for bed, you get scared and can't settle down. When you finally get tired, come to my room, wake me up, and I'll lie down with you."

Yes, you need to lie down with your child. Remember that you're creating **positive repetitious conditioning** around bedtime that's positive, not negative. It's a process. When you're lying with that child, you're helping to soothe the child's anxiety. The child will calm down faster, and she'll sleep better. If the child wakes up, let it be okay for her to come to your room. Telling her it's not okay to come into your room is the worst thing you can do. It doesn't mean you'll never have a night of sleeping without the child in your bed again. But when you tell the child she can't come to your room, dysregulation kicks in, and she'll be more likely to stress out and run around the house. If she knows she can come to your room, she may or may not need to do so because you gave her that safety net. Create a **love-based relationship** where the child can come to your room.

This can be a laborious process, but you will find that in a short while, the child will stay awake for shorter and shorter periods of time. Continue to make this a positive repetitious experience.

Of course, when you lie down with the child, lie down with the intention of going to sleep. I know this can be hard for parents. You might be thinking, "I only have from 9:00-11:00 all to myself. Now, I have to share this time with my child?" Do it for two weeks. If it goes well, try it for 30 days because at the end of 30 days, you will see a remarkable difference. Before you know it, you will have your whole evening back. If you fall asleep with the child, it was sleep you needed anyway, right?

It's also okay for children to sleep with a night light. Whether it's a child with a normal fear of the dark or an adopted child with traumatic events that happened around bedtime, lights going off will trigger stress for many children.

One more thing: Never allow babies adopted from orphanages to cry themselves to sleep. Allowing babies to cry themselves to sleep is not a good thing because it exposes the brain to uninterrupted states of stress. The child is not crying to manipulate you. **The child cries because of feelings of fear and stress.** Ignoring a crying baby creates **negative repetitious conditioning.** The child will come to believe that when they signal for help, they cannot trust that anyone will come to soothe that fear. Can you imagine the kind of dysregulation you'll experience later with such a child? The brain of a baby is not capable of self-soothing, so the idea that the baby will learn to soothe itself is simply wrong. They need to trust others to be able to soothe them. So, let's finally put this damaging practice to rest.

BATH TIME

Bath time is another one of those dynamics that becomes conditioned. You already read a bath time case study in the introductory chapters. Just as with bedtime, you need to create **positive repetitious conditioning** in place of negative repetitious conditioning. What we know is that bath time is usually a negative time for these children.

For whatever reason, they become dysregulated. You might even try giving the child the opportunity to take a bath in the morning rather than in the evening. Making that choice may just allow the child to be regulated enough to take a bath effectively. One of the first things you want to do is **create regulation around the whole event.**

Maybe an hour before bath time, sit down on the couch, and turn off the T.V. in order to read a story. Don't turn the T.V. off just 2 minutes before taking a bath because this will no doubt evoke defiance. Turn the T.V. off early in the evening, or bring the child inside earlier in the evening to create an opportunity for regulation. Think twice about playing games at this time because it could work the kids up. If you think it might help because games have a beginning and ending, try it, but make your decision based on your child's personality. Communicate to the child that you know he gets stressed at bath time. Communicate that you will be glad to come into the bathroom and sit with him for awhile.

The mother of the girl who learned her child had been sexually abused in the shower immediately told her daughter she didn't have to take a shower anymore. Her daughter didn't have that specific link to contend with anymore, so she could start taking a bath. After positive repetitious conditioning and many experiences of taking a bath safely, the girl was able to take showers again.

Think also about the **sensory integration** that occurs with the experience of the water. Some children don't handle hot, warm, and cold like other children. Some children prefer cold water or lukewarm water over hot water. Steaming water isn't necessarily required to kill germs. Test temperatures with your child until you find the one that makes the child most comfortable.

Brushing Teeth

Brushing teeth is heavily tied into sensory integration. In fact, it can be painful for many children with a trauma history. When the amygdala is engaged, the child may be hypersensitive to all sorts of things like the toothbrush, your touch, the tag in the back of a tee shirt, or even your eye contact. In a state of stress, the child is trying to cut down sensory pathways in order to regulate.

The two times for brushing teeth with a child are usually in the morning and the evening. Why must it be done during those times? The circadian rhythms are directly connected to those specific times. Morning is about waking up, and bedtime is about going to sleep. These are difficult transition times even for children without trauma histories. If the child is too over-stimulated or hyper-aroused, the process of brushing teeth may be too much stimulation.

I encourage you to *vary the times* you have your child brush her teeth. The only reason we push to have our teeth brushed in the morning is because it's a routine we've learned. If we really wanted to brush for hygiene, we would do it three times a day. Brushing teeth provides negative repetitious conditioning for lots of children. So, try waiting until after breakfast or after school, or ask the teacher to tell the child to brush after lunch. Create variability in the teeth brushing schedule, and you will find that there's a time of the day when your child is much more flexible to the idea of brushing her teeth. More than likely, it will be a time when the child tends to be more regulated during the day.

Ask your child if brushing her teeth hurts. You may need to get a very soft-bristled brush or an electric toothbrush. Don't forget that the resistance is related to stress, that stress leads to fear, and that fear leads to defiance. As the parent, you must demonstrate the internal security to help your child regulate. This means breathing to regulate yourself, which will, in turn, help your child to regulate.

If you have unfinished business yourself about bedtime, bath time, and brushing teeth when you were a child, it's time to acknowledge it and work on regulating yourself during these times.

If you're using the 10-20-10 prescription (which I strongly suggest with these behaviors), encourage your child to brush her teeth after one of these increments of time. She will feel more regulated as a result, and you'll be more likely to get those teeth brushed without difficulty.

Chapter 8

———◆·◆·◆·◆———

PUBLIC HUMILIATION OF PARENTS

Almost every parent has experienced feeling humiliated by their children in a grocery store, a shopping mall, restaurant, or other public place. What can you to do avoid these embarrassing situations?

The first thing to keep in mind is that there's a tremendous amount of **sensory stimulation** in these public environments. Close your eyes, and envision walking through a grocery store or shopping mall. Envision that everything is coming right toward you. This is especially true if you're small. This kind of thing activates your amygdala, the fear receptor in your brain. For you as an adult, your hippocampus quickly tells your amygdala that these things won't hurt you. It makes it possible for you to block all of that out. Children, however, especially those with trauma histories, don't have that ability.

When such a child enters a store, for example, that child's sensory system is immediately bombarded, and they move into a state of hyper-arousal. This leads the child to hyperactive, fidgety, or aggressive behavior. The next thing you know, the child is running ahead of you, and you have a stress reaction as well. If this happens repeatedly, just the thought of taking the child to the grocery store will cause you to have a stress reaction. Bear in mind that if it causes *you* to have a stress reaction, it causes the *child* to have a threefold stress reaction. That's the power of **negative repetitious conditioning**. As soon as you start thinking about going to the grocery store with your child, your heart rate starts to increase. Imagine that heart rate at triple speed — that's your child. I'm not speaking literally here, of course, but it illustrates the intensity of your child's stress reaction.

Shopping malls are even more stimulating because there are many more people approaching and interacting, and it's much louder than a grocery store. Think about it. The stores are competing with one another, so they have to use more color and sound to entice you to come in and spend money.

What happens is that we get into these scenarios and act out the same things repeatedly. Pretty soon, it's what the child expects. For the child, the over-stimulating store is a fear-based place, so the child becomes hyper-vigilant to threats in that environment. It doesn't matter if it's a clerk who never saw this child before or if it's you telling the child not to touch the merchandise. Remember that your hippocampus makes adjustments in this environment. Your child's does not. So, anything is a potential threat, and the environment creates sheer terror for your child. You need to understand the depth of your child's fear.

You must begin to notice when you go into your own stress and fear response. Then, you access the upper level thinking part of your brain (your hippocampus) to think through it. You talk to yourself and say, "This isn't about me. This is about my child, and he's scared right now. I've got to calm down and help him."

When behavior becomes severe, you almost always observe a **trauma link** attached to it. This means that the parent has moved into a stress reaction as well and may have unfinished traumatic business from childhood about going to stores. Think about your own childhood experiences in stores and restaurants with your parents. What was that like for you?

Of course, not every child who acts out in restaurants or grocery stores has trauma attached to it, but the experience of being in the store or mall can trigger other areas of your child's being that have trauma attached to them. Whether or not you believe trauma is involved—with either you or your child—the child is over-stimulated in these environments. The behavior is not conscious or malicious on the part of your child. You've got to be "response-able" and be able to respond to your child's needs in these settings. Your child is essentially saying to you, "I'm not capable of maintaining regulation in these environments. They're too stressful for me. I need help. I can't handle these places."

HANDLING THE STORE/MALL ENVIRONMENT

1. So, what do you do? Before you leave the house or mention to your child that you're going to the store or the mall, **take 3-5 deep breaths. Inhale and exhale.** Then, say to yourself, "I feel scared, I feel scared." You may not feel scared right then, but allow your body an opportunity to have that reality presented to it. Then, go to your child and say, "Sarah, we're going to go to the store." Tell her that you know she gets stressed out when you go to the store, and tell her that you're going to keep her safe with you. Don't ask Sarah if she gets stressed out because she's no more aware of her unconscious fear than you are the majority of the time.

2. When you get to the grocery store, get out of the car, walk around, and open the door for Sarah. **Hold her hand** while you shop, and have Sarah help you do some shopping. Get a basket, and ask Sarah to hold onto one side of the basket, or ask her to push the cart for you while you hold onto the front of it. You might even play a little game and tell her she can close her eyes if she wants while she pushes the cart and you steer it from the front. This allows Sarah to cut off a **major sensory pathway.** It helps her to regulate in this environment when she spends a few minutes unable to *see* all of the things that over-stimulate her. You're also engaging her in a little bit of fun in the process. *Prac-*

tice this when you don't necessarily have anything to shop for. When you practice this and have a good experience, you're creating **positive repetitious conditioning**. Practice this while you walk up and down the aisles, and every once in awhile, tell Sarah she's doing a great job. Tell her she must be feeling really safe. Ask her if you're keeping her safe enough.

3. When you're finished, try a little communication. Ask Sarah what stresses her out most about going grocery shopping. You might be surprised. She might say, "Well, you always get stressed out. Why shouldn't I get stressed out?" The next day, go to the shopping mall, and take the same approach.

4. What happens if you get to the grocery store, and Sarah doesn't want to hold your hand, push the cart, or close her eyes? Have her get *in* the shopping cart if that happens. Sure, she might weigh 100 pounds, but here's something important to remember: You don't have to buy a month's worth of groceries. Put her in the basket, and don't spend longer in the store than her behavior shows she can handle. Your child may be able to go into a store for no more than 5 or 10 minutes. If you push it to 15 minutes, it's not going to work. If you try that, get mad, and the child has a tantrum in the middle of the floor, you've just created more negative repetitious conditioning. It's a step backward in your process, and if you continue with this negative repetitious conditioning, the store experience will never get better.

5. Monitor your child's development zone to determine what she can handle in these stimulating environments. If you have younger children who don't weigh much, you can carry the child into the store. Do this for two weeks, and you'll see a dramatic change. Practice it a few times, and then go shopping. If you can be consistent in practicing this for two weeks or 30 days, your child will start to learn that these environments aren't so stressful and scary after all. The more you listen to your child's nonverbal communication, the more you'll be aware of what your child can handle and cannot handle.

RESTAURANTS

When it comes to restaurants, you not only have a situation that involves an over-stimulating environment for the child, but a child with traumatic stress history may have trauma issues around food as well. I worked with a mother once with her own trauma around food. Just the thought of preparing lunch for her two children caused her to feel anxious. Her children did indeed become stressed at mealtime, but the anxiety stemmed from the mother's own unfinished childhood business.

The way to know if a child has food issues is to observe how they handle food at home. If mealtimes at home are harmonious, restaurant visits should be okay, too. What may happen, however, is **social anxiety**. This anxiety increases for parents in restaurant environments, and if you expect your child to perform in a certain way in a restaurant, the child's anxiety may increase, too.

1. So, when you take the child into a restaurant, use the concept of **containment**, which means that you keep the child very close to you. Hold his hand from the time you get out of the car until you get into the restaurant and walk through the buffet line. If you don't, he may become **hyper-aroused**, which might cause him to talk more and louder. He might even want to say "hi" to everyone and start touching people. These are some of the behaviors that can result from hyper-arousal.

2. During containment, you're able to discipline the child rather than punish him. In order to discipline (teach), put your arm around him and say, "Jonathan, we don't touch other people in the restaurant. They may get scared when you do that. It's okay to say hi, but we don't touch." This is effective discipline, but don't think that it will necessarily carry over to tomorrow. Don't just expect that he'll remember not to touch the next time. Even though he has the message embedded in his memory, his **short-term memory** may shut down when he goes into hyper-arousal. You'll need to contain him again until he can remember your direction.

3. Sitting next to the child at the table will help to regulate him in the over-stimulation of the restaurant environment. If the child starts to talk more and louder during dinner, put your arm around him. Bring your face down close to him and ask, "What is it, honey?" Talk to him quietly.

4. Before you go to the restaurant, tell him you're going and that you know he gets stressed out and scared. Let him know that you've become stressed and scared in restaurants, too. Tell him that you're going to do something different this time. You're going to be calmer yourself so that you can help him feel safe. Explain that you know there isn't anything to be afraid of but that our bodies don't always know that. When our bodies don't know something, they don't communicate to our heads. Touch your stomach, heart, and head as you explain. Tell him you want him to be safe and feel secure. Stay right by him to interrupt the dynamics of stress and threat in restaurants.

5. Remember that your child may not be able to sit in a restaurant for a whole hour. Even if your child is 12 years old, he may regress to the emotional age of 3. Then, when stress kicks in, he'll only have the attention span of a 3-year-old.

So, practice, practice, practice! **Be aware of when your own fear kicks in**. If your child doesn't want to hold your hand in the restaurant, he may be communicating that "this is too much." The best thing to do in that situation is to walk back out of the store or restaurant.

CRISIS MANAGEMENT

What happens when you're not mindful? All of a sudden, your child is running all over the place, going up to strangers, and humiliating you. Your first reaction may be one of fear, making you want to control the situation. You tell the child to come back to you, and it just makes the situation worse. When your child is demonstrating dysregulation, get his full attention by loudly whispering his name.

After you have the child's attention for a moment, turn and walk in the other direction. Walk to the other side of the restaurant or back out the door. If you can get his attention in the midst of his fear and dysregulation and move away from him, he'll see his safety figure moving away from him. That will unconsciously motivate him to follow you. Keep walking until you're in a place away from people. Then, sit down and look out the window. Don't even acknowledge that he's coming toward you. When he gets close, look at him, and whisper in a low voice, "I can tell that you're really scared and stressed out right now. You know, I wasn't thinking. If I'd been more mindful, I would have known that you've already been through too much today. So, sit here beside me, and help me figure this out. Should we stay here and get something to eat, should we go and come back later, or should we just go home?" Ask him because at that point when he's engaged with you, he's more regulated.

If he wants to stay, offer to hold his hand, and walk with him to order your food. Ask him to tell you if he starts to feel scared. That's crisis management. **Remember that the calmer person has the ability to calm and soothe the one who's more stressed out.** When you can be calm and respond rather than react to your child's behavior, you'll help him to regulate and be more effective in the environment.

Chapter 9

NERVE TWISTERS:
CHATTERING, CLINGING, AND WHINING

Children who exhibit what I call "nerve twisters"—behaviors that really twist your nerves into knots—often have trauma histories without a **regulated adult figure** who could engage them with those early pre-verbal garblings and babblings like goo-goos and ga-gas. The baby just went on and on with no parent to mirror and reciprocate. Think about a child who is left in a crib with no one to give them a bottle, pick them up, or sing to them. There's no **reciprocal communication** and interaction. What happens with this baby is it continues talking and babbling without getting anything back. Finally, the baby starts to cry, and even their crying isn't met with anything reciprocal. The baby's **internal senses** never learn security through communication with someone else.

CHATTERING

Chattering is a behavior that parents don't talk about a lot even if they've experienced it a great deal. There's little understanding of this behavior and a lot of needless embarrassment on the part of parents. When parents do talk about it, they usually say something like, "Well, she's just talking that way because she wants attention."

Remember that **children don't act out for attention; children act out because they** *need* **attention.**

Let's say the chattering child is now 8 years old. When stress begins, that child regresses to her fear barrier, regressing to the age of being in that crib alone. This child's emotional age could be 12 months old. In this situation, any active engagement with an adult could trigger the child into chattering behavior. When a very verbal 8-year-old engages in mindless chatter, it's not consciously directed. It's not even goal-oriented in a normal communicative way. The only goal is to get some **reciprocal security.** In the process of chattering, the child is trying to feel more secure.

If the child follows you around chattering, what is that telling you about how much true, genuine, authentic attention you're giving her? It can't be very much, or she wouldn't feel the need to follow you. Think about it. If a baby just lies there gurgling and chattering into thin air, who is there providing security? No one! So, when your child does this, it's very much an example of regressive behavior. It's like she's crawling behind you saying, "goo-goo ga-ga" even though she's talking about what Tommy did and what Sara did. Even though she's using verbal skills, it's just like behavior in the developmental stages, as if she's crawling behind you. What she really wants to say is, "Pick me up! Pick me up! I really need some security. I really need you to interact with me!"

So, you have to flip the script. Turn around, and metaphorically "pick up" your child. You might sit on the couch and say, "Honey, I can tell that you really need me right now. Talk to me. Tell me what's going on." More than likely, she's going to begin to stutter and not have anything to say. But don't stop there because you know she needs you and is seeking your soothing. She just doesn't know how to communicate that to you. So, go ahead and say, "Come here, and sit in my lap. Just let me hold you, and if something comes up that you want to talk about, you can tell me. Why don't you tell me about your day in school, how you've been sleeping at night, or how you've been feeling?" You're opening the pathways of communication when the child feels more secure.

Parents sometimes say if they give the child 20 minutes, it isn't enough. The child wants more and is never satisfied. Think about the child's possible trauma history. If the baby is being rocked for awhile, followed by the adult walking away, what does the baby do? If the baby's not asleep, it starts to cry because the baby wants to be back in the adult's arms where it feels good.

So, when we have a child who sucks up our attention, we say the child has an attachment disorder. Naturally, as soon as we decide it's enough and walk away, the child shows signs of distress. The problem is that we have left the child when he or she still needs security. Then, we blame it on the child and call it attachment disorder. We have to put in the time in this process for it to become easier for the child.

Sometimes, of course, you may try to engage your child, but he doesn't want to talk to you. In this case, the old paradigm tells us that the child in us is just trying to manipulate and control you. With the old paradigm, the parent can win, but the child cannot. If a child loses, the parent loses too. When a parent is told, "You have to be in control, and if this child is chattering to you, you've got to make them stop because you're not going to listen to that garbage," the child loses. And the parent loses, too, without realizing it.

So, what happens when a parent spends that 20 minutes and says, "I've got something to do now, honey, so we can't talk anymore"? The child goes back into the chattering. Then what? That's when the parent has to communicate from a parent's understanding. The parent has to say, "Come here, honey, and look at me." Put your hands on the sides of the child's face and say, "Honey, I love you so much. Everything is going to be okay. You think just because I've been listening to you for 20 minutes and now I've got something I have to do, I may never come back and listen to you again. Well, honey, that's just not true. I *will* be back. What I want you to do is tell me right now, 'I'm scared.' Say, 'Mom, I get scared when you walk away.'" Coach this child to communicate with his **unconscious**.

Remember that **the unconscious cannot stand up when the light of consciousness is shined upon it.** You are exposing that child's unconscious to his conscious.

A child has no understanding that he's scared when you walk away. If you ask him, "Are you feeling scared right now?" He'll probably look at you like you're crazy. He might say, "No, I'm just trying to talk to you, and you're not listening to me. You're not listening to me because you hate me." But that's just behavior coming out. Underneath that behavior is **fear**. When you encourage the child to say, "I'm scared," he begins to get in touch with his true feelings. Say, "Okay, let's practice it. You take some deep breaths. Now, I'm going to walk out of the room. Now, I want you to be really quiet. I'm going to walk out of the room for 2 minutes. Then, I'm coming back." Then, you leave for 2 minutes and come back: "Here I am! Now, tell me anything that you were thinking about, honey. Tell me anything you want." Then, let the child talk again. Then, you say, "Okay, honey, I'm going to go out again. I'll be back. I know you're really scared. Tell me, 'Right now, I feel really scared because you're leaving.' Go ahead and say it." Then, respond: "It's going to be okay, honey. I love you, and I'm always going to come back." You walk out of the room and wait 3-4 minutes before you come back. You're creating **positive repetitious conditioning**. Then, you'll encourage your child to come to you ahead of time and say, "Mom, I really need to talk because I'm feeling scared." We were not taught **emotional communication** in our society. We were taught only **cognitive communication. Mindless chattering is nothing more than cognitive communication being driven by an emotional state.**

CLINGING

Clinging is the same kind of dynamic as chattering. Remember that the hippocampus completed its development around 36 months old? What happens between 18 and 24 months is that all of a sudden, the little baby makes a major shift. The little baby makes a major shift from feeling safe to move to anyone to all of a sudden clinging vehemently to the mother. This is because the infant hasn't yet experienced **cognitive repetitious learning,** so it begins to register everything as dangerous. The amygdala kind of goes haywire, and the child exhibits no cognitive capacity as yet to *know* what's dangerous and what isn't. The amygdala simply reacts.

So, during this period of time, the baby becomes clingy. What happens if that child is adopted during this period of time or placed in foster care? Right in the midst of this very sensitive time when this child begins to determine that things are frightening, everything suddenly becomes truly frightening! It's terrifying because the security the child has been clinging to is gone.

Why do these behaviors twist the heck out of our nerves? When our children are crying, clinging, or whining, it signals our own amygdalas. It's a signal that's literally impossible to ignore. You can't ignore that signal because it's triggered in your physiology. So when that child is clinging and saying, "Don't leave, don't leave, don't leave," your amygdala is activated. When you're in that process of tearing that child away from your leg, it's an extremely stressful process because you're literally creating minor grief dynamics. You're in stress, so that's why the child continues crying, spitting, and throwing up when you leave. The reason you feel terrible after you leave is because you just created a grief reaction in your body. You just sent yourself into hypo-arousal, which is literally like a depressive response in your brain and body system.

Here's something else to think about. When the child is stressed out and clinging to you, the child is touching you. Touch is a *major* sensory pathway. Just being touched by the child in that moment makes you feel overwhelmed because you're already handling too much stress. The reality is that you want the child to let you go! You have to be mindful of your own stress reactions. You can take some deep breaths to become less reactive. Say to yourself, "I feel scared right now. I feel terrible because I have to leave my child at day care."

I've been working with an adoptee who becomes petrified with fear when her mother leaves the room. The mother is a 50-year-old woman who reflected upon her own past experience. She said, "I remember that school was terrible for me because I literally felt like I was going to die if I left my mom." It's the same dynamic on varying levels for children who are really clingy. The old paradigm would tell you the child is trying to control you, so push the child away and don't be controlled. Now, I'm telling you, *forget about control.* **The only time we seek to control is when we're stressed out and scared.**

The true essence of control is to be able to regulate and *influence* the behavior of another. It has nothing to do with *overpowering* the behavior of another. When you forget about control, you will find that you're most in control because you're not worried about doing things right or wrong. You're just going with your heart, which allows you to see the fear underlying your child's behavior.

A child who is clinging to you is a child who is terrified. Do you want to just push this child away? Ask yourself that question. If they're really scared, do you just want to push them away? What about when we take our kids to day care? What do they do? They cling and cry because they know we're going to leave.

For that child, you are his or her life. In the child's tiny, immature cognitive regulatory system, they believe they're going to die if you're not there. And it's no different when it's your 5-year-old who's clinging, your 9-year-old who's clinging, or your 14-year-old who's clinging. In stress, they've regressed to that time when their cognitive regulatory system was immature. It's their fear barrier and emotional age. The fear—no matter how irrational—is: "If you leave, I'm going to die."

Listen to the behavior. Children communicate through their behavior. Sit down with the child and say, "Honey, tell me what you're feeling right now. I want to know what you're feeling. Are you scared? What are you scared of?" I was told about a child who told his mother that he was afraid he was going to die if she left. He

CHAPTER 9: NERVE TWISTERS

thought she was going to die, too. Do you think hearing something like that changes a parent's paradigm?

I'm not saying that you have to completely redo everything about your life when this kind of thing happens. But you do need to create some opportunities for your child's emotional expression. Sit down with your child and say, "Honey, I'm listening to you right now. Tell me how scared you are. I know you're scared because you're clinging to me, and you think something bad is going to happen to you. Let me explain it to you. You think something really bad is going to happen. You think maybe I'm not going to come back, or you think something is going to happen to you."

You open up the communication when you help the child to understand, and you reassure the child by saying that if you leave, you will always come back. Just talking about it may not be enough, however. You may have to have some of those **positive repetitious conditioning experiences** where you take the child to day care and experience the clinging and crying. Then, you say, "Honey, I know you're really scared right now. Tell me you're really scared. Now what's going to happen is I'm going to leave, and I'm always going to come back. We're going to practice it. You stay right here. I want you to know you're feeling really scared. I know I'm feeling really scared, too." You walk out, and the child is crying, clinging, coughing, spitting up, and in a terrified, petrified state. You walk out for a minute, *and then you come back.* You say, "Look here, I'm back!" You pick up the child and soothe him. You say, "Now, we're going to try it again." The stress starts kicking in immediately. The terror sets in just that quickly. Remember that it's an **amygdala reaction.** Then, you come back 5 minutes later. Do it again, and come back half an hour later. Say, "I'm going to come back when the clock is right here."

One thing I also recommend for parents who have children who get terrified at school is to make it okay for the child to call you a couple of times during the day—once in the morning and once in the afternoon. A lot of times, just hearing that they have permission to do this will transform a child's educational experience. Some

125

schools are pretty asinine about that, and they don't always want to allow the child to call, even though it's an easy thing to do. What I tell parents to do in that case is to call the children. Call in the mid-morning and again in the afternoon. Say, "Hey, honey, I'm just calling to check on you. Just wanted you to know that everything is going to be okay." This immediately allows the child to feel some **internal security**. But in the interim, you just need to understand that that's what some children struggle with. That's the essence of **attachment**.

Whining

A whining child is literally whining that she needs a **time-in**. The underlying meaning is, "Please, please, I need some time-in!" The child you see on the playground who's moping and whining is actually *screaming* for someone to create some regulation for her.

Similar to chattering, the **auditory stimulation** of whining causes our own amygdalas to react. It twists our nerves, and we say, "Please, just *stop* whining!" We just want to get the child to stop. We want to give them a lollipop to stop whining or put them in front of the television—anything. We want to get away from them because it stresses the heck out of us.

When your child starts whining and begging for your time, you have to stop and offer that time whenever possible. I know it isn't always possible—not for me either. Let's say my daughter is whining. If I'm in the middle of my work, I'm not always able to just stop and give her the time she needs, but I'm getting a lot better at it. Every time I practice it, it's **positive repetitious conditioning** for both of us. When this happens, I say, "Honey, I'm working right now." She goes away for about 5-10 minutes. Then, she whines and whines and whines. Finally, I take some deep breaths, and being mindful of my own feelings, I say, "You know what? Come here. Sit on my lap. What's going on?" She may not need anything more from me than to just be held and rocked in my chair. How long does it take? Just a few minutes—maybe 3-5. Then, she starts to calm down and says, "Daddy, will you come out and play?" I say, "Yeah, sure, I'm going to come out and play. You give me 20 minutes. I'm going to finish this, and then, I'll come out and play." And she's fine.

If I say, "Stop all that whining!", I create **negative repetitious conditioning** that only causes more whining. She **internalizes** everything, gets a little depressed, shuts down, goes into her room, cries, and then comes back whining a bit more about something she wants. The whining continues to escalate, so every time she approaches me in that hypo-aroused state, I create more stress for her if I say, "Go find something to do and leave me alone." When I do that, there are no learning opportunities and no positive repetitious conditioning.

It's no different than with a small baby. When a small baby starts to whine, it eventually ends up a full-blown cry. If you pick the baby up and soothe them when they start to whine a little bit, they don't go into a full-blown cry. Later, when they fall asleep, you put them down, and maybe it happens again. Maybe it happens again and again and again. But you just continue to pick the child up. That's what being a parent is about. If you do this, what happens when your son is 3 years old or 5 years old? When he gets a little frustrated, he may have a tendency to whine, but his regulatory system has learned through positive repetitious conditioning that it's okay to whine. So, he learns to soothe myself. He soothes himself because his parents taught him that. We don't learn to soothe ourselves through neglect. We learn it through positive repetitious conditioning. This is offering the child some really effective regulatory interaction. Children with this kind of interaction may begin to whine, but the behavior rarely grows into a full-fledged temper tantrum.

When your child begins to whine, just take 5 minutes. Train yourself that when your child is whining, you're going to take 5 minutes to give him your undivided attention and find out what's going on. Then, you can communicate to him, "You know, honey, I've really got to finish this work. It's not that I don't love you because I love you very much. So, as soon as I finish this, I'm going to come and play with you. We're going to do really fun things, but I need this time until then. Understand?" Get him to shake his head affirmatively. Say, "Okay, you go find something to play with. You know what? Why don't you get your toys and play over here close to me?" What are you doing then? You're creating containment for him and reducing his opportunities to get stressed out. When he stays close to you, he stays more contained.

Chapter 10

———◆•▶◀•◆———

No Eye Contact, No Touch, and Too Much Touch

Remember that any child's negative behavior is driven from an unconscious place of stress. If you have a child who won't make eye contact with you, who won't touch you, or becomes stiff as a board when you touch them, this child is in a place of stress and fear.

All of these areas: no eye contact, no touch, and too much touch have to do with an inability to regulate sensory stimulation. So, the first thing to realize is that you must avoid overloading the child with stimulation. Maybe it's night time, and you're using the affection prescription 10/20/10. You sit the child on your lap in the living room. You may have to turn down all the big lights and the T.V. By decreasing the sensory stimulation, the child can regulate more before you even put them on your lap. Another thing you can do is take the child into a room where it's just the two of you. You don't even have to talk. Just sit with the child because you're containing the space and decreasing the opportunities for over-stimulation.

No Eye Contact

Anytime you're working with traumatized children, especially if these children are labeled with an attachment disorder, no eye contact becomes one of those big behaviors that gets all kinds of negative stuff tied to it. We have been taught that if a child won't make eye contact, the child is trying to control you. We've been told that the child is trying to take charge. These beliefs are fear-based. So, let's look at it from a love-based perspective. Let's look at it from a **regulatory** perspective that accepts the neurophysiology of the phenomenon.

The eyes are the most direct, primary way that we stimulate the **frontal lobe** of our brains. That lobe of the brain is called the **orbital frontal cortex.** The significance of the orbital frontal cortex is that it's considered to be *our executive control center for our social and emotional functioning.* Along with the **hippocampus**, another part of the right hemisphere, the orbital frontal cortex directly affects our ability to calm our stress response system. When the orbital frontal cortex and hippocampus are overwhelmed with stress, it takes a gargantuan effort for the body to regulate and restore itself to balance. That's true for all of us.

Since our eyes are sensory pathways, a child in dysregulation must use every iota of his energetic being to move into regulation. Just looking into your eyes is overwhelming. Making eye contact when he's stressed out is probably one of the most overwhelming things that you could ask him to do. See this stuff in yourself before you try to see it in anyone else because when you can see it in yourself, you can see it more clearly in your child.

The next time you come home from work after a really stressful day, or the next time you get into a really aroused argument with someone, watch how little you make eye contact. One of the first things to go in the midst of stress is eye contact. Now, what do we know about traumatized children? They are extremely attuned to stress in the environment, which triggers their own stress reaction, which leads them into an emotional state of fear, which drives their behavior. And what's that behavior? Averting your gaze.

Are they averting your gaze to control you? Are they averting your gaze because they don't want to listen to you? No, they're averting your gaze because eye stimulation at that point could over-stimulate them to collapse.

Try talking on the phone while having a conversation at the same time with another person in the room. It will put your stress response system into overdrive. It's too much stimulation, right? This is how your child feels in an over-stimulated state.

Our regulatory system is what prevents us from going crazy with over-stimulation. But traumatized children don't have an intact regulatory system available to them. When the professional says, "You make that child look you right in the eye," the child looks at you completely blanked out. They have to do this because of an insufficient regulatory system. The hyper-arousal and threat is too great to *really* look at you. They need to move into **disassociation**, which involves blocking you and the conversation out, withdrawing, and freezing.

The first thing to do is move out of the paradigm that says there's something for you to be worried about if your child is not making eye contact. When your child fails to make eye contact, it's a strong message that he's feeling stressed. At that point, stop talking. Move to the child's side. Avert your gaze, and look in the same direction as his gaze. If he's looking down at the floor, you look down at the floor. When you move to his side, you're removing some of the stress. The first thing that happens when you **don't react** to his lack of eye contact is an opportunity for a more regulated environment.

Remember the negative feedback loop from the introductory chapters? Let me illustrate how it works in this circumstance. Take a piece of paper, and draw two stick people. Put your name above one figure and your child's name above the other. Suppose you say to your child, "Benji, I need you to clean your room," and Benji turns away and puts his head down. You just sent out a feedback loop. So, draw a little circle. When Benji puts his head down and doesn't respond to you, he send backs another feedback loop, so draw another circle around the first one. Then, you walk over to Benji and say, "HEY, DID YOU HEAR ME TALKING TO YOU?" You just created another bigger feedback loop around the second one. These are **negative feedback loops** because the dysregulation in the environment gets higher and higher. These negative loops can be avoided, and we can choose to create positive feedback loops.

A **positive feedback loop** works like this. You say, "Benji, I need you to do something for me," and Benji doesn't look at you. When Benji doesn't respond, he sends back a negative feedback loop because of his stress state. At this point, you have the choice to make the next loop negative or positive. At that moment, you must *stop and realize* that he's not making eye contact with you. So, you go stand beside him and put your arm around him if he can handle that. Stand beside him and avert your gaze to where he's looking. Then say, "Son, what's going on? I can see that you're struggling right now." Continue to look down at the floor with him. You just sent back a positive loop. He might mumble, "I don't know," which is a negative loop. Once again, you have a choice. So, you say, "I can tell that something is going on because you're not looking at me, and you're not really speaking to me. I can tell you're stressed out. Are you feeling overwhelmed about something? Do you want to talk about it?" He may say, "Well, not really." *But even at that point, the feedback loop is starting to change.* Then, you can say, "Listen to this, Son. Look at me." When you ask him to look at you, keep your gaze on the floor. When he looks at you, put your arm around him and say, "It's really important that we get this thing done." Don't look at him yet, but say, "I need your help." Then, you have the opportunity for real communication based on the positive feedback loop.

Then, you can communicate a sense of awareness and understanding to the child. Sit down with the child and say, "You know, honey, when you get really stressed out, you don't like to look at other people. And that's okay, because I don't either." In this case, you're not blaming or judging. You're empowering the child. You can say, "Honey, when you get really stressed out and scared, just let me know that it's too much for you to make eye contact right now, and I'll understand that." In this way, you educate your child.

The more positive you can be, the less his dysregulation will escalate. The more regulated **amygdala** has the ability to soothe the dysregulated one. The fear receptors in our brains communicate through vibrations to other people. The more you can maintain your positive state and encourage him to come out of his dysregulation, the more you'll be able to create a positive feedback loop. The negative will no longer be able to maintain itself in the presence of the positive.

Another example of this is when your smaller child is running around, and you say, "Come here, Sarah, and sit on my lap." She may be looking all over the place except at you. If you recognize that she's not looking at you because she's really stressed out and overwhelmed, you can pull her in a little more and start rocking her. You can say, "I can tell you're really excited right now." Sarah might squirm, so don't clinch down tighter. Loosen your grip on her. Then, say, "I just want to spend some time with you, honey." Even if she wants to hop up and bounce around and come back to you, that's fine. Then, just keep rocking her. You don't even have to talk that much. After some time, you can say slowly and gently, "Sarah, will you look at me?" Sarah may look at you, but it might be a fleeting moment before she looks away again. So, sit there a little quieter and longer. Then, say, "Honey, I really want to see your beautiful eyes, and I want you to see mine." Allow the process to take its course slowly and naturally. Don't force it.

What we have discovered is that when a child really wants to make contact with an adult, it's usually when the adult is engaged in something else. So, it's really the adult who's not making the eye contact with the child. The next time you go to the store, watch your own behavior when you get ready to check out. Watch how easy it is to not make eye contact with the clerk. It's so easy to feel that way because the store is so over-stimulating, even for us as adults. It's so overwhelming that we shut down. Anytime we can shut down a pathway to save us some regulatory space, that's what we're going to do.

NO TOUCH

When a child doesn't want to touch, it's the same dynamic as not wanting to make eye contact. The skin is the largest organ in the human body. When spread out, the skin weighs almost 16 pounds. It's the richest source of hormones throughout the entire body. It's through eye contact and touch that we have the most direct way to stimulate the brain. Smell is actually the most direct way to stimulate the amygdala, but eye contact and touch stimulates the rest of the brain most directly.

A child in a state dysregulation will stiffen up when you touch him because he feels overwhelmed and scared. This is when the body and the unconscious take over. As soon as your child stiffens up from touch, you know immediately that the child's sensory system is overwhelmed. The child's physiology is in a state of chaos, so he needs you to communicate with him in a very response-able, love-based way.

You might say, "I see right now that you're feeling overwhelmed. Come sit down on the couch with me. We don't have to touch. Just come and be close to me." You have to give the child some space, which is really hard for parents to do, especially when the child's stressed out. The parent's first impulse is to grab the child, but this is a fear reaction and a desire to make ourselves feel safe. Give the child space, and communicate that you understand by saying, "I can understand you don't want to be touched right now because you're feeling really scared. I'm going to sit on the couch, and when you start feeling a little bit better, you can come over and hang out with me."

I worked with a family not too long ago with a 9-year-old girl who got up and went into the other room, where she started arguing with her siblings. That told me immediately that she was dysregulated. I said, "Hey, Amy, come on back in here." She came back in and was obviously physically stressed out. You could see her anger, but of course, I knew that the underlying emotion was actually fear.

She said, "I don't want to go in there. I want to go out there with Ben." I said, "I understand that you do. But hang out in here with us for a little bit, and when you're feeling a little bit better, you can go back in with Ben." She didn't want to. She sat on the chair and said, "No," folding her arms. Her mother started to get up and bring her over to us. I said, "No, that's okay. Mom, why don't you and I just keep talking a little bit?"

So, Amy was there on the chair pouting, and I just raised my hand and signaled her to come over. She looked at me, still pouting. Mom and I kept talking, and Amy said, "I don't want to stay here. I want to go back and play!" I simply said, "I know you do, but I can tell you're really stressed out right now. So, we have to keep you safe and help you feel safe. Come back here with us, and when you're feeling a little bit better, you can go back in there to play."

She sat there a little bit longer while her mother and I talked. I could tell that this was an extremely frightened child. She was acting out her fear through the appearance of anger. Knowing that allowed me to remain calm and unthreatened by her behavior. If I increased the threat for her, she might have just gotten up and gone back into the other room. Because I remained calm and didn't increase the threat, she remained in the chair. My calm physiological state allowed Amy to be pulled into a positive feedback loop.

Finally, she looked at us, and I just patted the couch to motion for her to sit by me and her mother. Within 8 minutes, she sat between us. Amy was very sad, and it was an ideal opportunity for her mother to hold her and encourage her to talk about her sadness.

What made this work was (1) my ability to not become reactive and try to control the situation, and (2) my ability to allow her to remain in her state of dysregulation until the positive feedback loop I created was able to help her begin to regulate.

With children who have trauma histories, of course, touching can bring back terrible memories of abuse. Put your hands up right now, and say, "Don't touch me." Where do your eyes go? They immediately look away and toward the floor. You say "don't touch me" because in that place of stress, you're trying to save all of your sensory pathways. Eye contact is too stimulating in that moment of not wanting to be touched.

The other side of not wanting to be touched is a heightened degree of sensory pathway exposure. This is seen in children with **sensory integration** difficulties. The regulatory systems in some children are so impacted that certain pathways literally overwhelm them. These children struggle and struggle not to have those pathways activated. A lot of children experience problems with touch. A lot of children exhibit problems with hearing noises. A lot of children experience problems with different tastes and textures in their mouths. These are all different experiences of a heightened degree of sensory pathway exposure. A child with sensory integration difficulties is just a little bit more severe in their sensitivity. This child goes through the majority of the day not making any eye contact with anyone or goes through the majority of the day without touching anyone. These children are in a hypo-aroused category which causes them to want to shut down. When touch is forced on these children, they immediately shift to hyper-arousal and burst out in a negative way.

This is an example of the autistic child who moves into a corner, who doesn't want to be touched, and who doesn't want to look at anyone. He just wants to play with his papers or pens. We walk over and try to engage with the child, which sends him immediately into a state of hyper-arousal. A child who is in a state of hyper-arousal initially will switch to hypo-arousal when forced to make eye contact or touch. That's the only way the child can disassociate out of the over-stimulation.

When you have a child who doesn't like to be touched, you must encourage this child to sit on the couch with you. Suppose you say, "Honey, come over and get on my lap"? As soon as the child climbs into your lap, guess what you just did? You created *touch*. Touch doesn't have to entail your putting your hand on the child. You can just have the child get into your lap and lay your arms across him or her. You're already engaging touch.

If you have a child who doesn't like touch, get them a massage. You can give them the massage initially because a lot of the time, a child can handle the touching when he doesn't have the stimulation through his ears and through his eyes. A child can handle the physical stimulation when he doesn't have to deal with all of the other stimulation. If you can't handle giving the massage to your child, take your child to a professional massage therapist. The child is still getting that regulated activation, which is going to help his system start to get positive repetitious conditioning. The more positive experiences a child can have around something that's previously been negative and stressful, the better able the child will be able to regulate the next time.

TOO MUCH TOUCH

I once worked with a family who had a child who did the opposite — climbed all over the parents and touched them all over, including putting his hands in the parents' noses and ears. This family saw a professional who called this child's behavior "slimming." This therapist told them that they couldn't allow this behavior and should push the child away.

Simply put, this is a child who is in a state of stress and is actually **regressing** to the emotional age of an infant. Children who exhibit this behavior are either babies or children with very, very early trauma so that they regress to an infancy stage when in stress. They regress to that fear barrier. Your 8-year-old may even act in this way, touching you all over. It's called **exploration** in early childhood development. We love it when a baby touches our faces all over. But when an 8-year-old exhibits this behavior, that child is acting his emotional age rather than his chronological age. So, if you try to push the child away, guess what happens? It just creates more stress, and the child never moves out of that regressive state.

What I encourage parents to do is sit down, pull your child into your lap, and just let him touch you all over. Say, "Touch me all over my face, kiss my cheek and my nose and my face." You encourage him to explore you because every baby has done it. If you have a child with a trauma history, it could be that the child never had an opportunity to pass through this particular aspect of infant development.

As adults, we respond to this kind of touch with stress because we're very touch-phobic in our society. This phobia influences almost everything we do. The reason our society is phobic to touch is because it's stressful. We spend every single day feeling over-stimulated and trying to restore regulation, but so many of the things we do create more dysregulation and stress. Rather than just sitting still and listening to quiet music for a period of time, we go 100 miles an hour, watching television, smoking cigarettes, and drinking coffee. We may be trying to restore regulation, but unconsciously, we're creating more stress. When the child tries to explore you with touch, it's also an effort to regulate.

Chapter 11

POOR SOCIAL SKILLS, NO CONSCIENCE, AND LEARNING DIFFICULTIES

We usually classify poor social skills, no conscience, and learning difficulties as negative behaviors. This is unfortunate because these behaviors stem from immaturity and developmental irregularity. Such a child is in a state of stress. That stress gives root to the primary emotion of fear, which comes out as one of these behaviors.

Suddenly, the child is in a restaurant, rocking back and forth from the table, burping, stuffing his mouth very fast, and/or talking very loud. Even though we may tend to think of this as conscious behavior, I can almost guarantee you that at that level of behavior, the child has minimal or no awareness of what he's doing. Often, a parent says, "Honey, you're smacking and talking with your mouth full." The child then looks at the parent in utter disbelief because they're completely unaware. So, I suggest the parent then says, "Honey, you're rocking back and forth from the table. Are you scared? What's going on? Are you stressed out?" The child will likely stop the behavior and go back to eating. Making the unconscious behavior conscious—shining the light of consciousness on the unconscious—is a big shift which is literally like a physiological slap. You've probably experienced this as an adult. You might be at your desk with your knee bouncing up and down or chewing on your pen. Suddenly, you become aware of what you're doing and think, "Oh, my! What am I doing?"

No Conscience

When it comes to children who appear to have "no conscience," these children are, again, acting from a place of stress. It's a matter of survival for them, and they're acting from a very deep unconscious place. When a child is in a place of heightened stress and fear, and this leads him to behavior that pushes people out of the way, he demonstrates no conscious awareness of how his behavior affects these other people. He's acting out of a need to survive.

But what if someone runs toward the child and is brave enough to grab him and hold him for a minute? He'll probably freak out at first until he starts to calm down. The child might say, "I thought the big pit bull was after me. I was just running from the dog." It could be that the "pit bull" was just a Chihuahua. When someone points out that everything's okay and that the dog was just a Chihuahua, the child begins to come back to a more conscious place. Then, the child might see the people he pushed out of his way and feel ashamed. He might then go back and apologize because he's suddenly conscious of the behavior he just exhibited. But he wasn't conscious of it while it was taking place. In his mind, he was running from a pit bull.

Here's another example. I know someone who was in a hotel when the fire alarm went off in the middle of the night. Everyone tried to get down the emergency stairs and began to push other people out of their way in their fear. They wanted to survive and get out even though they didn't know if the hotel was actually on fire.

For each of us, our state level holds the **primal survival reptilian autonomic reaction.** That reaction is beyond cognitive thinking. In times of high stress, the outpouring of the amygdala bypasses the upper levels of the brain and goes right to the gut.

Can you see now why labeling a child as having "no conscience" is such a horrible label? The people who wrote the book that labeled children as such are functioning under a grave misunderstanding of human behavior. A child who *appears* to have no conscience is operating from a raw and core place of survival. **The child is in a pervasive life and death struggle.** Remember that physiology findings have shown that at times of stress, the cells of our bodies constrict into survival.

If your child appears not to have a conscience, please expand your heart and soul. Take a deep breath because when you breathe, you allow your body to move into a greater place of regulation. When you move into a greater place of regulation, you have a greater opportunity for a holistic balance that includes your body, mind, and spirit. This only happens through breathing. In the place of dysregulation, the brain, the heart, and the gut aren't connected. The only way to expand your heart and soul is to move outside of your own fear. As soon as a mental health professional tells you your child has no conscience, it triggers your own state of terror. It immediately makes you obsess about the future. Stress causes us to react from the past or obsess about the future. When both you and the child are in a state of terror, how can anything positive take place?

Remember that when we encounter a novel event or stimuli, we perceive that event as a threat until deemed otherwise. This is the state such a child is in when the behavior manifests. In survival, we freeze, and then, fight or flight kicks in. The child's unconscious says, "If I'm not frozen, I must fight. Therefore, when you come toward me, I have to attack you. Otherwise, you will hurt me."

A lot of parents wonder how that can be. How could your child not know that you won't hurt him? Look beyond your perception. **The only reason we view something as abnormal is because we fail to perceive it and understand it.** For a child acting from a place of trauma and terror, it doesn't matter who you are. Everything is perceived as a threat. Where do we see these dynamics playing out? They often happen at school. A child may hit someone and doesn't seem to care. What about children in juvenile detention centers?

Children break into an old woman's home, knock her down, and steal. Now, they say they really don't care.

Those dynamics are no different from the dynamics I talked about earlier with the people who pushed others out of the way when trying to get out of a burning building. When we're in survival mode, we don't care how other people see us.

IGNORE THE BEHAVIOR; NOT THE CHILD

So, the technique that I suggest is: **Don't approach your child about that negative event in that moment.** After the child hits someone or steals something and says he doesn't care, talking about how these acts are horrible or saying the child has no conscience will only increase the child's experience of threat.

The trick is to ignore the behavior, but not the child. When the child hits someone, and the other child's nose is bleeding, attend to the other child. Help that child calm down and regulate. Then, and only then, go to the child who did the hitting. Put your arm around him, and say, "Come with me. You must be feeling really scared" or "You look really angry right now. I know when you're angry, you don't feel very safe. Stay with me for a little bit because I know you're not happy that this just happened."

Why is it that we immediately assume that a child takes pleasure in a negative event? It's because we see those negative events as a threat, so we go into our own state of stress and fear. We're unable to see that the child acted out of a place of pain, not pleasure. Even if the child is laughing and pretending not to care, there's no real pleasure there. We assume the child took pleasure in the act rather than understand that the child acted out of a state of absolute terror.

Let's say I'm working with a child who acts out in this way on the playground. At the next recess, the child will stay a lot closer to me to try to keep himself regulated. I know that this child feels really threatened in the midst of all of the activity on the playground. In that stressed state, he doesn't have the ability to perceive that another child isn't a threat, so he hits his classmate. Then, he's so very frightened that he says he doesn't care that he's hit the classmate. At this state level, he actually can't care because he's in survival mode.

In this case, I would wait until the next day and say to him, "Tell me about yesterday. You were really upset and must have been scared. How you do think the child felt when he got hit? How did you feel about that?" Say this in a completely nonjudgmental way. The child may say, "I don't know." He may shrug his shoulders and put his head down.

How do you think the child is feeling at that point? He feels hurt and sad because now, he's connecting at an empathetic level. Until we are in a place of regulation, we cannot connect at an empathetic level. When we are dysregulated, we're not connected to our bodies or hearts. We can't feel anything but terror in that state. When we punish a child for his or her dysregulation, assuming the child has no conscience, we do nothing for the long-term picture.

So, I encourage you to create some space for the child to regulate himself. Then, you can become aware of how easily threatened he becomes. It could be that because of negative repetitious conditioning, the child goes into a heightened level of stress at the dinner table and says mean things to his sister. To change the pattern, you must become aware that this is what's happening. Rather than saying, "Don't say those things," don't say anything to him at all. Move to the sister, put your arm around her, and say, "Your brother really didn't mean that. He's just stressed out right now, but everything's going to be okay." Don't ask the boy to apologize because he won't be able to do so while he's still in a stressed state. Asking him to apologize will only trigger more fear and shame, and it won't evoke an authentic apology.

See your child beyond what mental health professionals may tell you. See the child's fear, and then, deal with your own. Then, ignore the behavior, but not the child.

If you have a 13-year-old acting like a 3-year-old, you need to respond to him as if he's 3, not 13. You might say, "Charley, wow, what's going on? Are you all right?" He might say, "No, I'm not all right because they aren't playing fair, and I don't like it! And I'm going to kill them. I'm going to kill somebody! I'm going to bring a gun to school and shoot everybody."

What do schools do when they hear that kind of thing? They immediately move into fear and kick the kid out of school to keep the school safe. The kid gets expelled, and the parents get blamed. We don't see and understand that this child is no different than any other 3-year-old, even if he *is* 13 years old chronologically. The only power he can garner at that point is to threaten everybody. That's the only way he feels safe. **Children who make such threats in times of stress are rarely going to follow through on the threat itself if they can just be provided an attentive, understanding adult willing to listen and process.**

The children who come back to school and act on the threat are the ones who were kicked out of school, punished for making the threat, and castigated for it. If you think about the Stress Model, it only makes sense, doesn't it? There's no understanding for the child, no regulation, and the threat just escalates until it explodes.

So, what that 13-year-old needs is a teacher or coach who will say, "Wow, you must be really mad! Why don't you hang out with me for a minute? Forget those guys. I can see things aren't going so good. Just come hang out with me, or better yet, I'm just going to hang out with you for a little bit." When we **recreate regulation in the midst of stress** for a child who is demonstrating poor social skills, we help that child to return his emotional age to a higher level of functioning closer to his chronological age.

Remember that children with a trauma history are more likely to have incongruent emotional, chronological, and cognitive ages. Even when they're semi-regulated, there will be incongruence. So, when they really move into dysregulation, there's going to be an even greater degree of incongruence.

BECOME PROACTIVE

When you go to family reunions or any place where there will be large groups of people, keep the child close beside you for at least the first 5-10 minutes. Just let them know that they need to hang out with you a bit to make sure everything's safe there. When you feel that the child has begun to calm down, give them a little freedom. You can say, "Okay, if you want to go play, go ahead. But I need you to check in with me every 5-10 minutes, or I'm going to check on you." Allow the child to play, and every 5-10 minutes or so, call the child's name or stand close to where he's playing. You don't have to engage him, but just let him know that you're standing there so that he can see you.

What you're doing is acting proactively and creating resonance of mind. This means you're triggering a reflective kind of memory engagement in the child's brain, allowing the child to continue to pull from his reserves of regulation just by seeing your face. We actually do this all the time. When we get really stressed out, we do it unconsciously. We automatically think of something soothing. We think of someone loving to give us a little bit more regulation. This allows us to continue to do what we need to do in an effective way. So, allowing the child to see you in these environments creates an opportunity for him to pull on some of those **regulatory reserves** and maintain his state of regulation.

Children with poor social skills are generally regressed 2-3 years emotionally even when they're in a state of regulation. When not regulated, they are regressed anywhere from 8-10 years below their chronological age. You have to keep this in mind. So, what do I suggest? **Encourage play with younger children.** As the child exhibits more positive interactive experiences with children without going too far out of their window of tolerance, the child will begin to grow emotionally. Wouldn't you rather your 10-year-old act like a 7-year-old when he's playing with other 7-year-olds and not when he's playing with 10-year-olds?

Environments with older children are more threatening, so the child is more likely to regress to his fear barrier. While the child plays with younger children, continue to check in with him every 5-10 minutes. A couple of things will happen because you're checking in and maintaining regulation for him. It will give him the opportunity to maintain a closer congruence between his chronological and emotional ages. As time goes on, this child will start to take more of an emotionally mature role in the group.

A lot of times, we see a child who likes to play with younger children, and we think he wants to do it in order to control the environment. On one level, that's true. But the desire for control is because the child is so desperately afraid. Feeling more in control helps him to feel safe. When a child feels safe, he will be more regulated, and his behavior will naturally be more mature because he hasn't regressed to his fear barrier. If he's playing with children who are chronologically and emotionally more immature than he, he'll naturally take on a leadership role. That is what you want to encourage and support because it means developmental progress is occurring.

I would even suggest that you play with the children. When two children are playing with one another, they can go on and on, remaining in a state of distress. But when an adult plays with them, the children find it easier to maintain regulation for a prolonged period of time.

That is why taking a child to a restaurant and teaching him how to eat with the silverware in a non-threatening way is very effective. More than conveying silverware skills, you're teaching him regulation first and foremost.

DEALING WITH SCHOOLS

If you're the parent of a child who is having these difficulties at school, how do you address the school to help the child? First of all, you must encourage the school to understand. If the child has a trauma history, the school needs to know this. The school needs to recognize that the trauma has caused the child to be very sensitive and scared. Let them know that when he's feeling sensitive and scared, he's prone to strike out at other children because he doesn't know what is safe. In his mind, he can't perceive there is no threat.

In this case, the school needs to be more proactive in keeping the child close to a teacher who has been instructed about how to talk to the child when he's scared. The school needs to keep the child more contained on the playground. As the parent, let your child know that you understand that he gets stressed out at school, and ask him to really work on telling the teacher when he feels scared. Help him with this at home by sitting him in your lap and having him tell you he feels scared. This will help him learn how to express his fear.

If the school continues to have difficulty containing the child, ask them not to let him go outside. A lot of schools look at this as punishment, but the other side is that when they don't contain a child, he might end up hitting someone. Then, he gets kicked out of school. You're being proactive in wanting your child to have the most effective school experience possible. If the playground is too threatening to your child, communicate to the school that he's too afraid and scared to play there, at least at this time.

Learning Difficulties

The bottom line is this: School is stressful. If you have a child with trauma history, school is more than just stressful—it's a threat. That means that school incites fear, which causes the child's thinking processes to become confused and distorted. Short-term memory is also suppressed. If you want to help this child overcome her learning difficulties in school, which may develop into a full-fledged learning disorder, you will need a tutor to help her with regulation. You may have a child who reads fine at home but struggles with reading at school. The significance is that when the child is regulated, her cognitive capacities are fully engaged in learning, but when she moves into a place of dysregulation, her cognitive processes are no longer as effective.

It's important to help the school personnel understand that the child needs something different in the classroom than the other children. Help the teachers to comprehend that she is to bring her school work home if that's what it takes. If possible, modify the child's schooling so that there's less homework. The child may have sufficient capabilities but shuts down in the stressful school environment and cannot function effectively there.

If you have a child with a trauma history, the school should create an IEP (Individual Educational Plan) to address some of these issues. Use some of my recommendations on education, and help this child's school process become more effective by modifying the school schedule. It might be helpful to switch to a smaller classroom and stop punishing the child when she fails to complete assignments on time. Putting that additional stress on her will just increase her dysregulation and cause her to shut down even more. Be aware that many things present as learning difficulties but have a **core origin of dysregulation**.

If helping your child with her homework causes you stress, it's best to get a tutor to help her regulate. You must be able to regulate yourself in order to help your child with school work.

Let's finally stop mislabeling these behaviors. If we do so and begin to truly understand the origins of these behaviors, we will give our children a chance to overcome them.

Chapter 12

Sexualized Behaviors: Masturbation, Perpetration, and Pet Perversion

This chapter contains very intense emotional content. Some of this information may be triggering for you on a very emotional level. So, if anything you read here becomes too overwhelming for you, please stop reading, and seek out someone you can talk to about what you're feeling.

Sexualized behaviors are some of the most severe behaviors that parents struggle with. It's a very intimate, frightening, and uncomfortable topic. It brings us into vulnerability and emotional exposure. It's important to realize, however, that **the great majority of children who act out these sexualized behaviors have had histories of sexual abuse.** It's highly unlikely that a child would act out any of these behaviors without having experienced a history of sexual abuse themselves.

It's also important to continue to remember that children acting out sexualized behaviors are driven from a highly and deeply embedded unconscious place.

Masturbation

This behavior can manifest at 2 years old up to 18 years old. For a child with a trauma history, the core dynamic of masturbatory behavior is that it's **self-soothing**. This behavior becomes **a self-regulating behavior**. When a child has been traumatized, sexual behavior has often been taught to them way too early and used in a negative way. Perhaps a 5-year-old had a 10-year-old sibling who would sneak into the 5-year-old's bedroom and masturbate them in the middle of the night. Stimulating the genitalia is a pleasurable experience in most situations, but the confusion for a child is that they're much too young to be experiencing this type of pleasure. They also can sense that the experience is somehow inappropriate. With very young children who act out masturbation, all the child learns is that it's pleasurable. The behavior is utilized when they're most under stress.

A traumatic experience is any stressful event which is prolonged, overwhelming, or unpredictable. Sexual stimulation is a stressful event. Sexual over-stimulation before you're developmentally able to tolerate, regulate, or actualize it is a traumatic event. Like all traumatic events, it embeds itself upon the **state level of memory**. Remember that the state level is the core level of memory where stress and trauma pervade. It's the instinctual level, and when sexualized trauma is perpetrated upon a child, it is embedded in the child's state level of memory. Therefore, when the child gets stressed and **dysregulated,** the young child (age 2-8) learns early that this pleasure isn't congruent with their age, physical, or emotional development. That traumatic event then becomes a **repetitive activity**. Any time the child is stressed, one of the first things they will do is self-masturbate.

For example, when a stranger comes to visit, a 3-year-old may sit in that stranger's lap and start humping back and forth. You may have a 5-year-old who watches T.V. in the living room and masturbates in front of everyone else. **At the earliest stages, these children have had this experience of pleasure tied into the experience of stress.** What they learn is that in times of stress, the most repetitive way to contend with that stress is through self-stimulation.

They don't have the emotional or cognitive abilities to regulate those feelings in a healthy, adaptive way.

By the time children reach the age of 8, they have more **social inhibition**. Masturbation for an older child is associated with shame. At this point, the child has more cognitive abilities to maintain a state of dysregulation without moving into masturbating behavior. The child demonstrates an enhanced ability to realize social settings that are inappropriate for such behavior.

When a parent sees a child engaging in these behaviors, two things can happen. The parent might feel shamed and become **reactive,** shaming the child. A trauma link doesn't have to occur in this situation. The parent may have no sexual abuse in his or her history in order to feel shamed. It's a societal reaction.

The second thing that can happen is that a lot of children with sexual abuse histories also have parents with sexual abuse histories. In this case, a trauma link does indeed occur. Through some dynamic that works through the unconscious, adoptive parents, foster parents, and many biological parents end up, from their sexualized histories, coming into contact with children who were sexualized themselves. Then, of course, the parent sees the child acting out sexually, and it immediately triggers an enormous reaction for the parent which ties into the parent's past sexual abuse. The parent might become extremely **hyper-aroused** and angry at the child, or the parent might shut down completely. This is very common for both children and adults with sexual abuse histories. In the midst of such overwhelming stress, the tendency will be to **disassociate** and go completely numb. That reaction becomes embedded in the state level.

What we have to realize is that this is a trauma-based, stress-driven behavior in small children. We also have to realize that for children without trauma issues, this can be on the continuum of normal behavior. It's within a range. It's not abnormal for any toddler to reach down and fondle himself. It's not abnormal for any 6-year-old boy to fondle himself from time to time. That is not masturbation. Masturbation is the activity directed toward orgasm or a peak level of pain. Some children, like adults with trauma histories, masturbate to incite pain upon the genitalia.

If you have a sexual abuse history yourself and have not yet integrated it, you will likely be triggered into your own emotional state around a child who exhibits sexualized behaviors. If your reaction leads you to immediately shame the child, it's likely that you haven't yet integrated your experience. It's important that the parent **see the act of masturbation as a sign of a deeper underlying state of stress.** The parent must listen to the behavior rather than shame the child or even immediately try to control the behavior. It's important to realize that this is a child communicating a deeper need. **Any child who continues to engage in this activity is still actively struggling with the sexual trauma.**

When you walk into your child's room, and your 6-year-old is masturbating, that child needs for you to take some deep breaths, not say a word, move toward her without even acknowledging what's happening, and sit on the edge of the bed. You want to say, "Sarah, I can tell that you're really stressed out and scared right now. Why don't you come and sit on my lap? Let me take you into the living room." I assure you that Sarah will stop if you do that. She may even stop as soon as you walk into the room because she'll have an immediate shame reaction. **The essence of shame is a fear of not being loved.** Shame is an intense and deeply felt emotional experience.

I suggest you move out of the bedroom because the bedroom at that age is associated with too much threat. Don't stay in that place. Take her in your arms to the living room and hold her, and ask her to tell you how she's feeling right now. Say to her, "Tell me how scary it must have been. Let me have your tears. Let me have your feelings." She will immediately start to go into her feelings, or she will immediately shut down. Hold her, and tell her that bad things happened to her when she was a little girl—very scary, hurtful things. Tell her that when she gets scared now, she acts out many of those same things because she learned that it felt good to her body. That was the only way she could feel better. Tell her she's too young to engage in that activity because "I can help you feel better. It's my responsibility as your parent to help you feel safe and secure, so you don't have to do that." Open up that communication.

The same dynamic goes for when you have a child who masturbates to create pain. Some small girls will masturbate with pencils, combs, or brushes enough to cause vaginal bleeding. These are children whose traumatic history was extremely painful. The process of self-stimulation for them must be heightened in order for them to reach a place of stimulation. If you see your child doing this, approach them in the same way. You cannot shame children out of masturbation. It doesn't matter how many times you've tried it or who says their behavior is wrong. If you shame children, they may stop in the moment, but the more you shame them, the more they will return to the behavior to try to regulate. The more you shame them, the more they move into dysregulation and need to engage in the only activity they know that helps them move toward regulation. **If your presence doesn't replace the child's need to masturbate by helping the child to regulate, you're not helping this child move past that traumatic experience.**

If you have a sexual abuse history yourself, and you find yourself becoming reactive to your child, you'll need your spouse to hold you and help you deal with your own emotions. I also encourage you to get some therapy. Find a therapist who understands the concept of regulation and dysregulation, and work through your issues around your own traumatic experiences. Your child will only be able to go as deep into their emotional state as you can bear to encourage them to go. If you are shut down emotionally while you try to help your child process this information, your child won't be able to open up either. You must get deeper insight into your own reactions in order to help your child.

I'm working with a mother right now who cannot hold her son because every time she holds him, he **regresses** to an infantile place and starts to touch her breast. Because she has a very traumatic sexual abuse history herself, she immediately wants to push him away. The dynamic is that he has a traumatic sexual abuse history as well, so both of them **reenact their trauma,** continuing the **negative cycle.** Therefore, I have encouraged her not to hold him. Instead, she sits beside him, gives him positive feedback about his behavior, and tells him how much she loves him. She can give him **back massages** because she feels comfortable with that. He lies down flat on his stomach where his hands aren't likely to reach up and touch her. I've encouraged her to give him two massages a day for 10 minutes each time because that's loving, non-sexual contact that he needs.

Then, once a week, I encourage her to hold him during the whole session in their therapist's office. The therapist gives her an opportunity to process the traumatic reactions for both of them, which creates positive repetitious conditioning for both parent and child. If they can do that consistently for three weeks or so in a therapist's office, this mother will be able to start holding this child again without having such an extreme reaction to his behavior.

PERPETRATION

When it comes to perpetration, there are two levels. First, we have to be concerned with the safety of others. Then, we have to be concerned with the safety of the child. I'm not talking about safety to others as a punishment to the child because even perpetration behaviors are a result of past trauma. No matter how severe you believe the behavior, the perpetrating child is still trying to achieve regulation through these acts. You only act out negative things from a negative place.

Children perpetrate on other children because they're stressed out, fearful, and terrified. The only way this child knows how to soothe that terror is to act out on other children to achieve regulation through perpetration. Children know that they can't perpetrate on an adult, but that doesn't stop some children from trying. If a child is extremely dysregulated, they'll try to perpetrate on whomever they can. It's that desperate for them. That's why in residential treatment centers, children with sexualized trauma histories try to perpetrate on everyone.

We sometimes think that children do this because they want to be powerful. "It's a power trip," we say. I don't believe that. I do believe they do it to control because they desperately need to control their environment as a result of extreme fear and dysregulation. They perpetrate on other children because it's a **traumatic reenactment** of a past event. It's an unconscious drive that recreates consistently and repetitively everything that happened in the past. When they've been sexualized, children learn very early how to create the activities which will bring them regulation in the midst of their dysregulation.

First, you have to address this child's core dynamics. You have to help this child to understand what's happening to him. Again, this cannot be approached with shame. Bring the child to you, and communicate. Say, "Honey, some really bad things happened to you. When you get really stressed out, you have a tendency to do really bad things to other children, and I know it makes you feel ashamed. It makes you feel guilty, and it scares you. I believe that sometimes, you probably believe that you can't control it." The reality is that when the state level kicks in, it often presents as uncontrollable. The behavior is only uncontrollable, however, because the child's consciousness has no access to what's happening in the unconscious. The child has no awareness of what he's truly feeling, and no alternative way to deal with his feelings.

You may have a child who's terrified at night time, which is more than likely when the traumatic experience occurred. So, this child needs regulation at bedtime. When we have awareness, we don't lock a child in their room at night. We don't put alarms on their door. This child needs a parent who's willing to lie down with them until they go to sleep, as well as get up and check on them several times throughout the night.

That's the commitment that it's going to take because just putting an alarm on the door will do nothing to reduce the terror and dysregulation the child experiences. **This child experiences as**

much fear and stress around night time as the children who are experiencing the perpetration. You must create safety for all of the children, including the one who is perpetrating.

If this has already happened in your home, communicate with all of the children about the dynamics that are occurring. Communicate that it's not okay to touch someone inappropriately. "However, we know that Johnny was touched inappropriately when he was young. Now, when he gets scared, he has a tendency to want to do it to others, but we're working on that." Then, you need to actively engage in the process of getting Johnny to experience, from an emotional place, the fear that he feels when he's dysregulated.

Of course, there is no space to ignore or deny sexual perpetration. You can't allow other children to be harmed. That's paramount. But the process doesn't have to be shameful. It has to be brought into awareness. **Create containment.** Johnny doesn't go in everyone else's bedroom. Process his feelings around night time, process his trauma, and process his tendencies at night time to seek security through the inappropriate activity with his siblings. Creating containment creates an environment of security for everyone.

If you have a fear that Johnny will get up as soon as you go to sleep, have Johnny sleep in your room on the floor, or sleep in his room with him. You have to be proactive and take the responseable approach. These are huge dynamics, and this is very serious. The other children in the home have to know that it's not okay for Johnny to come into their room. If he does, they must tell the parent immediately because as the parent, you're responsible for keeping everyone safe. This is not something to be brushed under the table. I've heard about too many adults who grew up in incestuous homes where their parents did nothing. They felt too much shame to be proactive. If you need therapeutic advice or support to handle the situation, go to a qualified professional. Just make sure you choose a therapist who will understand the true dynamics and not bring more shame or blame into your household.

If you have a feeling that your child was touched inappropriately, put the child in your lap, and tell her how much you love her. Tell her that there's nothing that can ever happen to her that will make you not love her. Tell her in a passionate way just how much she means to you and that you have a strong feeling that something bad happened to her. Tell her you need to know if that's so. If nothing happened, more than likely the child will be adamant that nothing happened. If she is truly adamant about it, you can trust that nothing happened.

If the child tells you that something did happen, make sure the child feels no shame about it. Let the child know that it's not okay for someone else to touch them inappropriately, but it's not their fault. They did nothing wrong.

PET PERVERSION

Children with trauma issues will often act out in a mean way with animals. Again, this behavior stems from the child's internal state of dysregulation. Situations like this can escalate especially if the dog is a little anxious. That anxiety provokes a stress interaction with the anxiety-ridden child. It can begin with simple petting, and as the petting increases, the animal starts to move away. The child then feels more anxious and moves toward the dog. Over a period of time, there is negative repetitious conditioning that creates an immediate stress reaction between the child and the animal. This child goes toward the animal instead of moving away from it.

When children act out sexual behaviors on animals (masturbating animals, sticking pencils in their rectum), it's usually directly connected to **reenactment of trauma**. The child is essentially acting out what happened to them on some level. The only way the child can **integrate** the trauma of the past is to understand on an emotional level what he or she experienced. When they begin to have awareness and insight about why they're driven to engage in these activities with animals, they can begin to integrate the past sexual trauma.

Again, it's important not to shame the child. Realize that **this is an opportunity to listen to this child who's communicating through his behavior that he's not in a good place.** Say to the child, "Paul, I can see right now that you're really scared about something." He's going to be in such a state of shock at that level. His system is already in a state of extreme dysregulation, and his state level is highly triggered. Ask him to give you his feelings about the situation, and tell him that you know it's only when he feels scared that he hurts the dog. Hold him, and encourage him to express his emotions. When you do that, you create the beginning of a positive repetitious condition that you can experience with Paul every single day. Create a dialogue where you can move from the emotional expression to just talking about what happened to him. It may not have to be every day, but begin talking about it. Then, you will start to **recondition** Paul and the family animal in a positive way.

Bring the animal over, and pet it to calm it down. Then, have Paul come over. Take Paul's hand, and ask him to take deep breaths. Say in a gentle, nonjudgmental voice, "We don't hurt the animals. Sometimes, interacting with the animal by yourself causes you a lot of stress. That leads you to want to hurt it. You can pet the dog, but masturbating the dog, sticking pencils in its rectum, or having it lick your genitals is not okay. When you're feeling that way, come to me and tell me." If you can get small children to communicate with you when they feel the impulse to have the dog "lick their peepee," you can then help to regulate the child in that moment of stress and prevent the behavior in that moment. You can hold the child, **tell him it's okay to have those feelings, and thank him for communicating his feelings to you.**

Once again, monitor your own reactions during this process. Is your own upbringing leading you to want to shame the child? Even if you don't want to shame the child consciously, **you may have unconscious impulses to shame the child because you would feel shame yourself in this situation.** If you feel an unconscious impulse to shame the child, you need to work on your own reactions within yourself. You need to work on regulating yourself in these circumstances.

Remember that this behavior is communicating, "I'm in a state of fear that I can't control and don't know how to handle. I need your help." If you address these behaviors directly, you will start to see amazing things happen to the child. **Remember that this is a child who is acting out of vulnerability and who needs security from you.**

TEENAGERS

Let me address teenagers who engage in masturbation. First of all, it's natural adolescent behavior to start to explore the body. You simply need to watch for evidence that the exploration is becoming deviant. This would be in the case of a teen who starts to masturbate in public or engage others in the process. When you see those kinds of deviant activities, you have to assess if there's trauma in the child's history.

Begin by opening up communication. You can say, "Look, Sam, I noticed that the other night when we were at dinner, you were masturbating yourself under the table. This is significant because it tells me that the environment at dinner was too stressful for you. It also tells me that at some point, you learned that this was the best way to soothe yourself. We need to process this."

As difficult as it is, it's important that you let the adolescent know that you know the masturbation is occurring. If the child feels scared, let them know it's okay for them to come and talk to you about it. Let them know that it's a **natural reaction,** and if there's trauma around it which is leading them to have shame, you want them to communicate with you about it. Let them know that this shame might lead them to engage in behaviors that are painful. It's important that you communicate to the child that it's a natural activity but that it must be done in appropriate settings.

If you're dealing with a child who's emotionally delayed,

however, that child may not have sexual trauma in their history. The behavior could be caused by the emotional delay, such as some form of mental retardation. In that case, the child may become over-stimulated in certain environments and immediately move to that self-soothing activity from a completely unconscious place. In fact, the child may have no conscious awareness that it's inappropriate in that setting. So, again, shaming is not only unnecessary, it's pointless and damaging. It simply becomes a matter of teaching the child what's appropriate.

It's important to heal our own shame about sexual behaviors. In order to integrate these traumatic experiences, we need to become comfortable with sexuality within our own beings. Only then can we help our children to develop healthier sexuality for their adult lives.

FINAL WORD

————❖————

I know this book is a lot to digest. Some of the behaviors you will never encounter, thank God; others will be daily reminders of the impact of stress and trauma on the development of a child.

Painfully, you will need to read it again. Repetition is how you create concrete learning. Because this is new paradigm information, you must commit to repetition. Don't give up—give in. Accept the pain that has not been of your making but is now your responsibility. It is a blessed work you are doing, truly the only genuine work that matters to fostering peace in the heart and in the world.

Don't be afraid to ask for support or help. There are more good and wise therapists out there than bad, but don't be afraid to run from the bad. Give your therapist this book and have him or her read it and see how they react. Can they support you? Help you honor your own fear and anxiety while nudging you slowly forward into love?

Don't be afraid to take a break and send your child to a friend for a weekend. You might be surprised that his behaviors are not nearly as challenging for a weekend at a friend's house as they might be at home. Just remember to let your friend know that your child is stress sensitive and fear-full.

If things at home get really scary, don't be afraid to call the police. We all need a greater intervention sometimes. The key is to learn from each experience and to not give up. There is no such thing as failure; there is only giving up or not being willing to take a fresh look, question, and challenge your old beliefs and experiences.

Return to this book not as the end all and be all in dealing with these severe behaviors but rather as a guide and companion through a challenging process of healing. Remember that every behavior is an outcome and to best change outcomes we must analyze the process leading up to each. I have provided key insights into the process but you have the knowledge, wisdom, and understanding of your child to determine which corrections you need to make to continually push love forward into the heart of your child and home.

I'm here for you and I believe in you and know that love heals all. Send me your questions, your successes, and your failures. I want to know.

In the meantime...here's to love.

May God bless and keep you and your child safe during these challenging healing times.

Bryan Post

RECOMMENDED READINGS & RESOURCES

Resources for Parents & Professionals:

Brazelton, T. B. & Greenspan, S. (2000). *The Irreducible Needs of Children: What Every Child Must Have to Grow, Learn, and Flourish.* Cambridge, MA: Perseus Publishing.

Brazelton, T. B. (1992). *Touchpoints: Your Child's Emotional and Behavioral Development.* Reading, MA: Addison-Wesley Publishing.

Breggin, P. (2000). *Reclaiming Our Children: A Healing Solution for a Nation in Crisis.* Cambridge, MA: Perseus Books.

Clark, N. & Post, B. (2002). *The Forever Child I A Tale of Lies and Love.* Upland, CA:. The Forever Child. Available www.postinstitute.com.

Clark, N. & Post, B. (2003). *The Forever Child II A Tale of Fear and Anger.* Upland, CA:. The Forever Child. Available www.postinstitute.com.

Clark, N. & Post, B. (2005). *The Forever Child III A Tale of Loss and Impossible Dreams.* Upland, CA: The Forever Child. Available www. postinstitute.com.

Clark, N. (2005). *The Forever Child IV Family Secrets: A Tale of Silence and Shame.* Upland, CA: The Forever Child. Available www.postinstitute. com.

Davis, P. (1999). *The Power of Touch: The Basis for Survival, Health, Intimacy, and Emotional Well-being.* Carlsbad, CA: Hay House.

Divinyi, J, M.S., L.P.C. (2001). *The ABC's Workbook: Achieving Acceptable Behavior Changes.* Peachtree City, GA: The Wellness Connection. Available www.postinstitute.com.

Divinyi, J, M.S., L.P.C. (2003). *Discipline That Works; 5 Simple Steps.* Peachtree City, GA: The Wellness Connection. Available www. postinstitute.com.

Divinyi, J, M.S., L.P.C. (2003). *Good Kids, Difficult Behaviors.* Peachtree City, GA: The Wellness Connection. Available www.postinstitute.com.

Fox, E. (1934). *The Sermon on the Mount: The Keys to Success in Life.* San Francisco: Harper Collins.

Goleman, D. (1994). *Emotional Intelligence: Why It Can Matter More Than IQ*. New York, NY: Bantam Books.

Granju, K. & Kennedy, B. (1999). *Attachment Parenting: Instinctive Care for Your Baby and Young Child*. New York, NY: Pocket Books.

Hart, A. (1992). *Stress and Your Child*. Dallas, TX: Word Publishing.

Kabat-Zinn, M. & J. (1997). *Everyday Blessings: The Inner Work of Mindful Parenting*. New York: Hyperion. Available www.postinstitute.com.

Karen, R. (1994). *Becoming Attached: Unfolding the Mystery of the Infant-Mother Bond and Its Impact on Later Life*. New York, NY: Warner Books, Inc.

Karr-Morse, R., & Wiley, M.S. (1997). *Ghosts from the Nursery: Tracing the Roots of Violence*. New York: Atlantic Monthly Press.

Kuchinskas, S. (2009). *The Chemistry of Connection*. Oakland, CA: New Harbinger Publications. Available www.postinstitute.com.

Liedloff, J. (1986). *The Continuum Concept*. New York, NY: Penguin Books.

Perry, B. D. (2006). *The Boy Who Was Raised As a Dog: And Other Stories from a Child Psychiatrist's Notebook*. Cambridge, MA: Basic Books. Available www.postinstitute.com.

Post, B. & Forbes, H. (2006). *Beyond Consequences, Logic, and Control: A Love-Based Approach for Helping Children with Severe Behaviors*.

Post, B. & Grantham, S. M.S., M. Ed. L.P.C. (2005). *Going Home: A Survival Toolkit for Parents*. Palmyra, VA: POST Publishing. Available www.postinstitute.com.

Post, B. (2003). *For All Things a Season*. Palmyra, VA: POST Publishing. Available www.postinstitute.com.

Post, B. (2005). *Healing Adult Attachment Handbook* Vol.1. Palmyra, VA: POST Publishing. Available www.postinstitute.com.

Post, B. (2005). *How to Heal the Attachment Challenged, Angry and Defiant Child: When Behavior Modification and Consequences Don't Work* (DVD). Palmyra, VA: POST Publishing. Available www.postinstitute.com.

Post, B. (2009). *How to End Lying Now!* Palmyra, VA: POST Publishing. Available www.postinstitute.com.

Post, B. (2009). *How to Heal the Attachment Challenged, Angry and Defiant Child: When Behavior Modification and Consequences Don't Work – Bryan Post's New Family Revolution* (Workbook). Palmyra, VA: POST Publishing. Available www.postinstitute.com.

Post, B. (2009). *How to Heal the Attachment Challenged, Angry and Defiant Child: When Behavior Modification and Consequences Don't Work* (Online Course – POST Online Learning Center). Palmyra, VA: POST Publishing. Available www.postinstitute.com.

Post, B. (2009). *Parenting Softly: From Infant to Two.* Post Miracle Parenting; a Subsidiary of Miracle Industries, LLC Rio Rancho, NM www.miracleblanket.com. Available www.postinstitute.com.

Post, B. (2009). *Stress, Love & Your Baby's Developing Brain:* Understanding How Your Parenting Approach Influences Your Baby's Brain Development From Prenatal to Two. *(DVD).* Post Miracle Parenting; a Subsidiary of Miracle Industries, LLC Rio Rancho, NM: www. miracleblanket.com. Available www.postinstitute.com.

Post, B. (2009). *The Great Behavior Breakdown.* Palmyra, VA: POST Publishing. Available www.postinstitute.com.

Post, B. (2010). *From Fear to Love: Parenting Difficult Adopted Children.* Palmyra, VA: POST Publishing. Available www.postinstitute.com.

Post, B. *Adoption Subsidy and the Law: What Every Parent Needs to Know.* (CD Audio Recording). Palmyra, VA: POST Publishing. Available www.postinstitute.com.

Post, B. *Bryan Post's Adult Attachment Seminars* (CD Audio Recording). Palmyra, VA: POST Publishing. Available www.postinstitute.com.

Post, B. *Dr. Bryan for the Family Live Radio Show* (11 CD Audio Recording). Palmyra, VA: POST Publishing. Available www. postinstitute.com.

Post, B. *Educating Children Today: Working with the Difficult Child in the Classroom* (DVD). Palmyra, VA: POST Publishing. Available www. postinstitute.com.

Post, B. *Effective Strategies for Severe Behaviors in Adoptive and Foster Children* (DVD) Palmyra, VA: POST Publishing. Available www. postinstitute.com.

Post, B. *Getting Started with Bryan Post: A Journey Toward the Family-Centered Way for Parents* (CD Audio Recording). Palmyra, VA: POST Publishing. Available www.postinstitute.com.

Post, B. *Great Behavior Breakdown* (13 CD Audio Recording). Palmyra, VA: POST Publishing. Available www.postinstitute.com.

Post, B. *How to End Lying, Stealing and Defiance in Children* (DVD). Palmyra, VA: POST Publishing. Available www.postinstitute.com.

Post, B. *IEP's and the Law: What Every Parent Needs to Know.* (CD Audio Recording). Palmyra, VA: POST Publishing. Available www. postinstitute.com.

Post, B. *International Adoption Course Ages Birth to Five* (12 CD Audio Recording). Palmyra, VA: POST Publishing. Available www. postinstitute.com.

Post, B. *Stress, Trauma, and the Secret Life of Your Child* (CD Audio Recording). Palmyra, VA: POST Publishing. Available www. postinstitute.com.

Post, B. *Understanding & Meeting the 9 Most Important Emotional Needs for Foster & Adopted Children* (DVD) Palmyra, VA: POST Publishing. Available www.postinstitute.com.

Purvis, K. & Cross, D. (2007). *The Connected Child.* New York: McGraw Hill. Available www.postinstitute.com.

Rosenberg, M. (2003). *Nonviolent Communication: A Language of Life.* Encinitas, CA: Puddle Dancer Press.

Sears, W. & Sears, M. (2001). *The Attachment Parenting Book : A Commonsense Guide to Understanding and Nurturing your Baby.* New York, NY: Little, Brown and Company.

Siegel, D.J. M.D. & Hartzell, M. (2003). *Parenting From the Inside-Out: How a Deeper Self-Understanding Can Help You Raise Children Who Thrive.* New York, NY: Jeremy P. Tarcher/ Putnam.

Siegel, D.J. M.D. (1999). *The Deloping Mind: How Relationships and the Brain Interact to Shape Who We Are.* New York, NY: Guilford Press. Available www.postinstitute.com.

Siegel, D.J. M.D. (2008). *The Mindful Brain: The Neurobiology of Well-Being.* (CD Audio Recording). Boulder, CO: Sounds True Inc. Available www.postinstitute.com.

Siegel, D.J. M.D. (2008). *The Neurobiology of "We".* (CD Audio Recording) Boulder, CO: Sounds True Inc. Available www. postinstitute.com.

Simon, R. & Roorda, R. (2007). *In Their Parent's Voices: Reflections on Raising Transracial Adoptees.* New York: Columbia University Press.

Tolle, E. (2005). *A New Earth: Awakening Your Life's Purpose.* New York: Plume

Additional Resources for Professionals:

Bowlby, J. (1969). *Attachment and Loss: Vol. 1 Attachment.* New York, NY: Basic Books.

Bowlby, J. (1973). *Attachment and Loss: Vol. 2 Separation and Anger.* New York, NY: Basic Books.

Bowlby, J. (1980). *Attachment and Loss: Vol. 3 Loss: Sadness and Depression.* New York: Basic Books.

Bowlby, J. (1988). *A Secure Base: Parent-Child Attachment and Healthy Human Development.* New York, NY: Basic Books.

Bremner, J. (2002). *Does Stress Damage the Brain: Understanding Trauma-Related Disorders From a Mind-Body Perspective.* New York, NY: W.W. Norton and Company.

Carnegie Corporation (1994). *Starting Points: Meeting the needs of our youngest children. The report of the Carnegie Task Force on meeting the needs of young children.* New York, NY: Carnegie Corporation of New York.

DeGangi, Georgia. (2000). *Pediatric Disorders of Regulation in Affect and Behavior.* New York, NY: Academic Press.

Frattaroli, E. (2001). *Healing the Soul in the Age of the Brain.* New York, NY: Penguin Books.

Greenspan, S., and Cunningham, A. (1993, August 22,). Where do violent kids come from? *Charlotte Observer,* reprinted in the *Washington Post.*

Janus, L. (1997). *Echoes from the Womb.* Livingston, NY: Jason Aronson.

Justice, B., & Justice, R. (1990). *The Abusing Family.* New York, NY: Plenum Press.

Kagan, J. (1994). *Galen's Prophecy: Temperament in Human Nature.* New York, NY: Basic Books.

Kandel, E. R. (1998). A new intellectual framework for psychiatry. *American Journal of Psychiatry, 155,* 457-469.

LeDoux, J. (1996). *The Emotional Brain: The Mysterious Underpinnings of Emotional Life.* New York, NY: Touchstone.

Levine, P. A. (1997). *Waking the Tiger, Healing Trauma.* Berkley, CA: North Atlantic Books.

Levine, P. A. (1999). *Healing Trauma: Restoring the Wisdom of the Body* (Audio Cassette Recording). Louisville, CO: Sounds True, Inc.

Lipton, B. (2005). *The Biology of Belief: Unleashing the Power of Consciousness, Matter, and Miracles.* Santa Rosa, CA: Mountain of Love/ Elite Books.

McEwen, B. (1999). Development of the cerebral cortex XIII: Stress and brain development—II. *Journal of the American Academy of Child and Adolescent Psychiatry, 38,* 101-103.

McEwen, B. S. (1992). Paradoxical effects of adrenal steroids on the brain: protection vs. degeneration. *Biological Psychiatry 31,* 177-99.

Montagu, A. (1986). *Touching: The Human Significance of the Skin.* New York, NY: Harper and Row.

National Center for Clinical Infant Programs (2005). *Diagnostic Classification of Mental Health and Developmental Disorders of Infancy and Early Childhood.* Arlington, VA: Zero to Three.

O'Brien, P (2008). *Unconditional Commitment: The Only Love that Matters to Teens* (DVD) Palmyra, VA: POST Publishing. Available www.postinstitute.com.

Perry, B. D. (1996). *Maltreated Children: Experience, Brain Development, and the Next Generation.* New York, NY: W. W. Norton.

Perry, B. D. (1996). Neurodevelopmental adaptations to violence: How children survive the intergenerational vortex of violence. *Violence and Childhood Trauma: Understanding and Responding to the Effects of Violence on Young Children,* Gund Foundation, Cleveland, OH.

Perry, B. D. (1997). Incubated in terror: Neurodevelopmental factors in the "cycle of violence." In J. Osofsky (Ed.), *Children in a Violent Society* (pp. 124-149). New York, NY: Guilford Press.

Perry, B. D. (2002). Childhood experience and the expression of genetic potential: What childhood neglect tells us about nature and nurture. *Brain and Mind, 3,* 79-100.

Perry, B. D. (in press). Neurodevelopmental aspects of childhood anxiety disorders: Neurobiological responses to threat. In C.C. Coffey & R. A. Brumback (Eds), *Textbook of Pediatric Neuropsychiatry.* Washington, D.C.: American Psychiatric Press.

Perry, B. D. (Spring 1993). Neurodevelopment and the neurophysiology of trauma: Conceptual considerations for clinical work with maltreated children. *The Advisor, American Professional Society on the Abuse of Children, 6:1.*

Perry, B. D., Pollard, R.A., Blakely, T.L. Baker, W.L., & Vigilante, D. (1995). Childhood trauma, the neurobiology of adaptation, and "use-dependent" development of the brain: How states become traits. *Infant Mental Health Journal, 16* 271-291.

Pert, C. B. (1997). *Molecules of Emotion.* New York, NY: Touchstone.

Pert, C. B. (2004). *Psychosomatic Wellness: Healing Your Bodymind* (Audio CD Recording). Magic Bullets, Inc.

Pert, C. B. (2004). *Your Body is Your Subconscious Mind* (Audio CD Recording). Boulder, CO: Sounds True, Inc.

Post, B. *Creating Healing for the Attachment Challenged Adult* (Audio CD/ DVD Recording). Palmyra, VA: POST Publishing. Available www. postinstitute.com.

Post, B. *Family Regulatory Therapy for the Attachment Challenged Adult, Child and Family* (DVD). Palmyra, VA: POST Publishing. Available www.postinstitute.com.

Post, B.. *Art of the Family–Centered Therapist: Fear and the Dance Between Therapist and Client* (Audio CD Recording). Palmyra, VA: POST Publishing. Available www.postinstitute.com.

Ross, C. A. (2000). *The Trauma Model.* Richardson, TX: Manitou Communications.

Sapolsky, R.M. (1990). Stress in the wild. *Scientific American 262,* 116-23.

Schore, A.N. (1994). *Affect Regulation and the Origin of the Self.* Hillsdale, NJ: Lawrence Erlbaum Associates, Publishers.

Schore, A.N. (2003). *Affect Regulation and Disorders of the Self.* New York: W.W. Norton.

Schore, A.N. (2003). *Affect Regulation and the Repair of the Self.* New York, NY: W.W. Norton.

Shapiro, F. & Forrest, M. (1998). *EMDR: The Breakthrough Therapy for Overcoming Anxiety, Stress, and Trauma.* New York, NY: Basic Books.

Siegel, D.J. M.D. (1995). Memory, trauma, and psychotherapy: A cognitive science view. *Journal of Psychotherapy Practice and Research, 4,* 93-122.

Siegel, D.J. M.D. (1999). *The Developing Mind: How Relationships and the Brain Interact to Shape Who We Are.* New York, NY: Guilford Press. Available www.postinstitute.com.

Smith, E., Clance, P., & Imes, S. (1998). *Touch in Psychotherapy: Theory, Research, and Practice.* New York, NY: The Guilford Press.

Sroufe, L.A. (1996). *Emotional Development: The Organization of Emotional Life in the Early Years.* Cambridge, UK: Cambridge University Press.

Sroufe, L.A. (1997). Psychopathology as an outcome of development. *Development and Psychopathology, 9,* 251-268.

Valenstein, E. (1998). *Blaming the Brain: The Truth about Drugs and Mental Health.* New York, NY: The Free Press.

Praise for the Great Behavior Audio CD Program

I am a foster mom who was desperate for help until I received The Great Behavior Breakdown CDs. I only take the most severe behavioral children between the ages of 5 and 12. I also had adopted a child 14 years ago who was a heroine/crack baby. For so many years I saw the fear under all the behaviors but I didn't always know how to handle or understand the situations. I also knew their brain's didn't process like children without trauma. This information has and will save the lives of the children I currently have as well as many more. I have never seen any techniques work so well and so quickly as the ones I have learned. I have had to deal with every behavior you speak of. My only regret is that I didn't get this information sooner.

Many nights I cried and prayed to become a better parent. You have answered my prayers to reach these children.

My community is desperate for help, and as I learn now and practice these techniques on my children I am sharing with others. I have a great concern for the growing number of children being adoptive and then returned, young children being sent to treatment centers and, the number of different placements in foster homes, all because no one knows how to deal with these children. My goal is to open a short term group home using only your techniques while educating parents, teachers, foster and adoptive parents.

I found the answers to every question I ever asked on how to help my child overcome her fears and behaviors. In every session I listened to you described the behavior of someone I have cared for and gave me simple ways to help them. Love does conquer all fear. I would like very much the parenting articles to share with others in my community. God Bless you so much.

Thank you
Sheila

Would You Like More Help? Immediately? Free?
We have lots of excellent material covering many
aspects of Parenting Challenging Children — for Free!

Visit us:

- www.bryanpost.com — Bryan's blog offers weekly insights, tips, and other resources. You can even sign up to have these blog posts emailed to you directly.

- www.facebook.com/postinstitute — for daily inspiration, insights and the chance to interact with other parents, professionals and the Post Institute. Like us and get a free copy of Bryan Post's How to End Lying New e-Book.

- www.youtube.com/postinstitute — Choose from a library of stored videos, many of them less than 10 minutes long but offer a wealth of information.

- www.twitter.com/Bryan_Post — What is Bryan thinking right now? Also latest email updates.

- www.linkedin.com — Contact Bryan directly.

- www.postinstitute.com — Sign up for our totally FREE weekly Parenting Series

- www.postinstitute.com/free–stuff — videos, audio recordings & interviews, articles and FREE e-Books

- www.postinstitute.com/AttachmentDisorder — Learn about our Parenting Attachment Challenges Children "Hands-On" Home Study Course. Effective, Easy interactive design with hours and hours of video and reading materials with a fully illustrated fill-in-the-blank workbook. Affordable, and comes with a *100% Peace of Mind "Iron-Clad No Questions Asked"* Unprecedented 12 Month Guarantee!

- www.oxytocincentral.com — Presents the latest information and resources on the powerful "love" hormone oxytocin. This naturally produced chemical can help heal and ease the pain for children from hard places, and for the parents that love them.

INDEX

group home 5, 22, 169

H
hippocampus 31, 35, 78, 79, 82,
     109, 110, 120, 128
hoarding 93–97
holding hands 71–72, 74, 111,
     113–115
homework 86, 146
humiliation 109–115
hyper-arousal 28, 31, 35, 55, 60,
     62, 65, 68, 71, 76–78, 82–84,
     87–89, 102–103, 110, 114,
     129, 133, 139–142, 145, 150,
     166
hypo-arousal 28, 31, 35, 55, 60,
     62, 65, 68, 71, 76–78, 82–84,
     87–89, 102–103, 110, 114,
     129, 133, 139, 140–142, 145,
     150, 166
hypothalamus 94, 102

I
IEP 146
ignore behavior 41, 59–60, 140
Individual Educational Plan 146
integration 45

K
Kabat-Zinn, Jon 30
Kabat-Zinn, Myla 17, 30

L
learning difficulties 137, 145–146
life and death struggle 57, 139 *See
     also* survival
light of consciousness 30, 38–39,
     44, 64, 66, 120, 137
Logic and Control 18, 53

love 27, 36, 42–43, 50–53, 104,
     150, 155, 160
     against fear 42, 50
lying 57–60

M
massage 135, 152
masturbation 147–152, 157–158
     to incite pain 150–151
mealtime 93, 97–99, 102,
     113–114
memory 29, 35, 49, 58, 113, 143,
     145, 148
     four levels 30

N
Nardoni, "Gestapo" 17
negative feedback loop 39–43,
     129–130
nerve twisters 117
neurophysiologic loops 37–43,
     80, 101
night light 105

O
O'Brien, Pat 17, 20, 22
opposition defiant disorder 54
orbital frontal cortex 128
orphanage 77, 96, 105
overeat 94. *See also* gorging

P
pain 2, 61, 140, 150, 151, 159
paradigm shift 26
perpetration 152–155
Perry, Bruce D. M.D. 30
Perry, Dr. Bruce 77
pet perversion 155–157

About the Author

Bryan Post is an internationally acclaimed therapist, speaker, and author. He lives in a small town in Oklahoma with his family where he enjoys sitting on the back porch watching the birds and the leaves dance in the wind.